A Debt REPAID

My Debt for a Medical Education to My Father, the U.S. Army, Charity Patients, and God, and How I Repaid Them All In Forty Years

CURTIS D. BENTON, JR., M. D.

TATE PUBLISHING, LLC

ISBN: 1–5988615–2-2

Dedicated to the graduating class of 1945,
Emory University School of Medicine

FOREWORD

True modern medicine really began in the early 1940s. Surgical techniques made great strides as the injuries sustained by soldiers in World War II were treated; bacterial infections began to be conquered with the new antibiotic, penicillin; understanding of hormones and the isolation of cortisone changed the way many diseases were handled; medical research advanced on all fronts; and American physicians entered enthusiastically into a new era in which the patient was the primary concern of the doctor. Patients were aware of, and appreciated, the relationship. Doctors loved their patients, and patients loved their doctors. There was little or no insurance to cover medical expenses, and patients paid what they were able to and were charged according to their ability to pay. The poor were treated free, and doctors actually made house calls. Those idyllic years lasted less than four decades, but they were medicine's Golden Years.

I was privileged to undergo the metamorphosis that takes place as a student moves through a medical internship and eventually becomes a physician. Most of the events described in this account actually occurred. Names, dates, and some details have been changed in the interest of continuity and better story telling.

I also entered this rigorous experience period as an atheist but emerged as one who found his way back into the Christian fold with a new and maturing understanding and commitment.

In addition, by the time I had completed an internship and a residency in the speciality of ophthalmology and otorhinolaryngology (eye, ear, nose and throat),

I realized that I was deeply in debt, not financially, but personally and emotionally.

CONTENTS

PREFACE

What does it mean to have a heart for service? How can you tell if someone has such a heart? How does it show in them? It shows in a thousand ways; in the things they do, in the things they don't do, in plans they make and the plans they break. I know, because I've seen this up close and personal, for this describes my father.

Patients can tell if a doctor is genuinely delighted to see them when they encounter him at the mall or if he'd rather they'd not enter his personal space when he's not in the office. Because once he allows them in that space, they just might show him something that really hurts and he just might end up back at the office peering through the slit lamp. But the next time they see him at the airport they'll be even more excited! This, too, I've seen in stores and airports all over the country and even around the world—loving patients who never forget.

Having a heart for service is more than allowing your plans to be altered to meet the needs of others in your path. It's also changing your path to encounter others with needs, seeking out people to serve. Not only has Dad said "yes" when people have asked, he's searched for places where the need is so great that the people could not ask.

I just know you're going to enjoy this book, reading the entertaining stories, and getting to know my father, a wonderful man, who truly has a heart for service.

Dudley James Benton, Ph.D.
Knoxville, Tennessee

CHAPTER 1
A DEBT INCURRED

**To my father, the U.S. Army, the patients on whom I
learned my skills, and to God**

My father paid my tuition for my first year at
Emory University School of Medicine. I lived at home, a
short distance from school and an easy walk each morning to class. My father had no expectation of my repaying him, but left that task for me to do the same for any
children I would have in the future, for he was able to
cover the expenses of my schooling as he had done for the
four years of college preceding medical school. Our family was blessed enough to be part of what is considered
the upper-middle-class. We owned our own home, had
a paid-for automobile, and even enjoyed household help
five days a week. School tuition was not an extreme burden. I did, however, have an opportunity to do something
special for him seventeen years later—more about that to
come.

My second year expenses were paid by Uncle
Sam, as my entire class was inducted into the Army in
1943 and continued on in our education. The burden on
my father was immediately reduced to room and board
only. The Army, knowing physicians would be needed in
the armed forces as well as the home front, arranged to
assume the expenses of doctors-in-training in exchange
for our services later when our education was complete.
There was an extra benefit to me and my classmates in the
category of "unexpected consequences." As more practicing physicians were called into military service, a period of
unprecedented opportunity to gain hands-on experience

in our training that exceeded anything before in history. This period became known as the "see one, do one, teach one" era in which we were forced to learn quickly and seriously.

The final two years of school was completely paid for by my gaining the job of emergency x-ray technician that provided room and meals in the teaching hospital, Grady Memorial Hospital in Atlanta, Georgia.

The Army was willing to wait for its payback until I had finished the residency—more about that later.

The professors and instructors through the school years didn't expect any pay back from us students. They received salaries for their work, but there were ways we students could and did show our appreciation for their outstanding efforts on our behalf. Our professors gave generously of their time and talents, and our class developed some strong bonds with them. We were able to honor some of our teachers at class reunions in subsequent years.

During internship and residency, also accomplished at Grady Hospital (affectionately known as "The Gradies" because there existed in the 1940's two Grady Hospitals under one administration, a hospital for whites and one for blacks, then called "colored"), I received room and board in the hospital plus a salary: ten dollars each month the first year, twenty the second, forty the third, and a whopping seventy-five bucks the final fourth year. Having so much income, I felt able to get married that last year to one of the hospital's dieticians with whom I had fallen in love. That's probably one of the reasons I'm still alive and healthy at age 84, because Margaret prepares and serves me delicious and healthful meals.

Those years I also became indebted to two different groups of people: the attending staff of dedicated and talented visiting physicians and second, the great number of uncomplaining patients who entrusted me with their health, their eyesight, and often their very lives. The details of my internship / learning period still remain vivid in my memory and are worth recounting in some detail.

The other "person" who gives continually in all aspects of my life is my maker and sustainer, the Lord God. It took me a long time to become aware of my debt to God, but through the years that obligation and relationship has grown and become more precious year by year.

How was I to repay all to whom I was indebted? It would take more than forty years to square the score with everyone, and I'll try to explain how I've done it.

CHAPTER 2
LEARNING IN THE ADVENTURE
OF INTERNSHIP

1945-1946

July 1945

When I had graduated form medical school, my mother and father had moved to South Florida. I had spent a week at home with them after graduating from medical school.

"What does all this Latin mean?" Mother asked when I proudly unrolled the parchment for her approval.

"It means I am now allowed to take the State Board examination and start my internship. A year from now, I'll be ready to serve my time in the Army and eventually come back here to be a real doctor."

After my mother, Evelyn, called to her husband, "Come out to the swing, Hon, and I'll read you Junior's letter."

Curtis, Sr., an individual whose thin frame gave his 5 foot 10 inch height the look of a taller man, smoothed his thinning, brown hair over the bare dome of his oval scalp and tossed a pillow onto the white porch swing. He often sat on the wood slat swing in the afternoon to watch the sun sink into the western horizon. It was a pleasant time to reflect on the events of the day and enjoy the gorgeous pinks, reds, and purples of the sky as the hues all finally faded into blackness.

Evelyn unfolded the stems of her reading glasses, rested them on the bridge of her thin, smooth nose and opened the white envelope.

The years had been kind to Evelyn Benton, who at forty five, retained her long blonde hair, not yet showing grey, gathered neatly at the nape of her neck, and a girlish complexion that was never given the opportunity to be damaged by the harmful sun. Her body was tall and trim, showing no spread in spite of bearing two children. She read slowly and clearly, her voice musical from many years of singing in the church choir.

Dear Mom and Dad,

Well, I'm finally here at the huge Bi-County Hospital. Patients and staff alike call it "The Gradies." I've been assigned to a large open room with three other interns.

Bill Andrews lives in Chattanooga, and he has already invited me to visit him at Lookout Mountain on one of the holidays – if we get any time off, that is. Do you remember the story about the society lady from Atlanta who took her maid to the top of Lookout Mountain and told her she could see five states from where she stood? The maid said it wasn't true, because she couldn't see the yellow, blue, orange, and red colors that the states have in a geography book.

Lewis Collier comes from Tampa, Florida. He went to medical school in Alabama, there being no medical school in his home state of Florida. Says he wants to be a bone doctor. Dad, he reminds me of that saying: "Big enough to go bear hunting bare handed."

Arnold Burnside grew up in Mobile. He also got his M. D. in Birmingham. He talks so slow it's even hard for a Southerner to understand him. He can make "yes" into a three syllable word! He says he hopes to be either a family doctor or a pediatrician.

By the way, Bill's not sure what he's most interested in. He'll see what he likes during our rotating internship. Our first four months will be on the surgery service.

I don't have to wear my Army uniform any more. All I need now are the white pants and little white jacket with the hospital name printed on the pocket. I also get free meals and ten dollars cash every month. I have to work six days and five nights a week, so I probably won't have time to spend the ten bucks, except for toothpaste, shaving cream, and razor blades. I'm glad I never took up smoking or chewing gum.

Haven't heard from the State Board exam yet, but I think I passed. They say that those of us who plan to stay and practice in Georgia usually get a passing grade.

And thank you for the nice leather Bible you gave me for graduation. You remember how, in my freshman year in college, Professor Ruck insisted that the Bible was just a collection of writings of ancient folk tales and interpretations of events after the fact. I quit reading it after that course. Now I don't have time to read it, even if I wanted to. One thing Professor Ruck did say has stuck in my memory since then. When some parents complained to Professor Ruck about his "tearing down the Bible," he challenged them to read the Pentateuch straight through and tell him if they really thought one person wrote the entire thing. A month later, the parents returned and said they couldn't find a book called the Pentateuch in their Bible. Using that couple's ignorance as a claim that Moses didn't write the first five books of the Bible is a pretty weak argument. Professor Ruck used it as a joke to tell the class, and everyone laughed. Now I think it was just unkind. I know you both were upset when I turned to atheism in college, but I thank you for still loving me and praying for me. I love you both. I'll write each month - more often if I can.

Love,
Curtis, Jr.

Evelyn slipped off her glasses, folded the letter, and reached to her husband's knee.

"Hon, how is it that someone as smart Junior, top of his class from high school through medical school, came to believe that God doesn't exist and the Bible is not important?"

"Young people are very impressionable in college," her husband replied.

"They are learning so many things that they think they can understand the nature of the world, and the world of nature, through their own limited reasoning. They don't consider the unseen world that's all around us. Even people who worship idols realize there are forces that can't be seen which affect our lives."

"I'm not giving up hope on Junior," Evelyn replied. "God will make Himself known to our son. We'll just keep praying and believing."

Grady Hospital stood four stories high in two red brick buildings, bisected by a city street. A short flight of steps, ending under a rounded arch, led into the visitors' reception and administrative offices. The building for white patients, with its emergency room facing a side street, had floors of rooms divided into wards, such as surgical, medical, and obstetrics. A separate, two story edifice housed pediatrics. A large magnolia tree, revered symbol of the deep South, filled the small plot of grass by the front sidewalk. The enormous white blossoms contrasted with its dark green, leathery leaves each spring and early summer.

Opposite the white hospital stood a similar rectangular structure that housed the colored patients. The wards, rooms, and facilities were an exact duplication in both buildings. Although the doctors were all white, their time was divided equally between the segregated patients in the two buildings. A broad tunnel under the street connecting the two was frequently used during inclement weather or at night. Winters in Atlanta, though not intensely cold, presented many grey, dreary days. Proper snow covered the ground only two or three times a year, and it usually melted within a few days. Almost every winter, when the thermometer stood at the freezing mark, rain would solidify into ice when it came in contact with tree limbs, power lines, homes, and street surfaces. Known as "ice storms," these oddities of nature brought misery to the city residents as tree limbs crashed down onto roofs, power lines, cars, and streets, creating hazards for vehicular and pedestrian traffic. The hospital tunnel was especially appreciated at these times.

I lived at Grady Hospital my last year of medical school because I had been chosen as one of two students to operate the x-ray machines for emergencies once the salaried technicians went home at night and on weekends. My transition from student to intern did not involve a change in either sleeping quarters or uniform. But with my internship I would be involved in real doctoring at all hours of the day and night instead of just taking x-rays. An advantage of the student job was observing the patients and learning what diagnosis and treatment followed the results of the x-rays.

Late one July afternoon, my roommates Bill, Lewis, and Arnold, and I were sitting on the plain wooden benches in the surgeon's dressing room on the second floor of the white hospital. The elective surgery for the day had been completed. A nearby hamper was filled with several sets of green surgical outfits that had been haphazardly tossed there by the residents and visiting doctors after they changed into their street clothes. A three tiered rack held an assortment of blood stained tennis shoes, loafers, scuffed and cracked oxfords that served as operating room footwear after being declared unsuitable for public or private use.

The four newest interns were recounting events of the past few days when a tall man with gold-rimmed glasses, a brown three-piece suit, and a brown felt hat entered the room. He reached up to a metal beam that spanned the toilet stall and ran his fingers along the top. Bringing down a dusty coin, he said, "If the orderly ever cleaned this room the way he should, he'd be rewarded with this two bits. But I doubt he'll ever wipe the dust off that spot.

"By the way, gentlemen, I'm Dr. David Elkhart, professor of surgery, and I'm here to teach you new doctors how to wash your hands."

We four young men introduced ourselves and changed into green hospital scrub suits.

"They're supposed to have a variety of sizes," Dr. Elkhart said, "but they usually only have two sizes, too small and too large."

As he slipped on a pair of raggedy brown loafers from the shoe rack, he added, "You'll each need an old pair of shoes to keep here and another for the colored O. R., but for now, just slip on anything that fits."

The fivesome pushed through the large swinging doors marked SURGERY - NO ADMITTANCE EXCEPT AUTHORIZED PERSONNEL. To their right was a cubicle for the nurse supervisor, who sat at her desk, completing the records of the day's operations. On the wall adjacent to Mrs. Rose's desk hung a large chalkboard, divided into squares with information on the four operating rooms, the nature of the surgery, the time schedules, and the names of the surgeons and patients. The circulating and scrub nurses were identified by written initials.

To the left, two large sinks projected from the wall, and over each extended a single faucet, like an inverted "J", with long paddles on either side that could be pushed by one's elbows to control the flow of hot and cold water. A shelf above each sink held several scrub brushes, half floating in a yellowish liquid disinfectant. Beside each sink stood a tall contraption that ejected liquid soap from a nozzle when pressure was applied to a foot pedal. Droplets of green soap liquid, and a few bubbles, gave evidence that the floor had not yet been mopped since the last surgery less than an hour before. Opposite this were the four swinging doors of the operating rooms themselves, a hidden world of mystery soon to become familiar haunts for the four young men who now looked anxiously around.

"You boys think you already know how to wash your hands," Dr. Elkhart began, "but scrubbing for surgery is different. There are millions of common germs on our hands all the time, hiding under our fingernails, in the creases of our skin, and on the surface. Your job is to get rid of most of them. Germs usually can't penetrate intact skin, but when we cut through that wonderful protective covering that God gave us, we expose tissues that germs love to attack. If those pesky critters get in a wound, even a clean surgical wound, we can kill some of them with sulfanilamide powder, but it's much better to keep them from getting into our surgical incisions in the first place.

"Of course, you'll wear sterile rubber gloves, but sometimes holes develop, so the hands must be as near sterile as possible. Before rubber gloves, doctors worked with bare hands. What's more, the eye surgeons still do, because the gloves interfere with the delicate touch that's required. It amazes me how they can handle those tiny sutures and instruments.

"Back to the business at hand—you'll learn all about sterile techniques, but today we start with hand washing."

Pointing to Lewis, Dr. Elkhart asked him to step over to the sink. He took Lewis' hands in his own and looked at his fingernails through the bifocal part of his glasses.

"Always keep your nails trimmed short," he said.

The respected doctor then took a black pen from his scrub shirt pocket and began making large dots on Lewis' hands and arms all the way up to his elbow.

"These marks will not come off with water, but they will disappear with soap and brush scrubbing. I'm going to put a blindfold over your eyes, ask you to scrub at that sink for five minutes and see if all those marks are gone."

With his eyes covered, Lewis lathered and scrubbed both hands and forearms. Dr. Elkhart stopped the intern after five minutes were up. Removing the cover from Lewis' eyes, he said, "Rinse off the suds and let's see if any black marks remain."

Much to the surprise of the others of us, and to Lewis' chagrin, two spots were visible on each forearm, and two more between a pair of fingers on his right hand.

"It's not as easy as you thought, is it?" the professor said with a sly grin. "Let me show you fellows a few tricks."

Dr. Elkhart demonstrated how to use the pointed metal nail file that rested in a basin of germicide. As he cleaned under each nail, he frequently placed his fingertips and the file under the running water. With the brush, he carefully worked between each finger and methodically attacked the front and back of each hand and forearm, rinsing often. He then watched with hawkish eyes as each of us novices carefully followed his example.

"That's enough for today, doctors; I'll see you same time next week," he concluded.

Later, walking back to our room, Arnold quipped, "If someone asked what we learned today, it would sound funny to say we learned how to wash our hands, wouldn't it?"

"Dr. Elkhart has a reputation for being an exacting and demanding surgeon," Bill said, "but he was very pleasant and patient with us today."

Lewis and I stopped by the mail cubicle to look for letters.

"You know, Curtis, that hand scrubbing is a lot like life, isn't it?" Lewis said.

"How do you mean?"

"Some people try to appear so clean on the outside, yet they have some hidden, dirty spots in their lives."

"We're all human, Lewis, a mixture of good and bad."

"Well, there was one perfect life in history," Lewis said, "Jesus Christ."

"But wasn't he a man like us, Lewis? He must have done some bad things or at least had some bad thoughts," I said.

"He wasn't just like us, Curtis. He was perfect."

I decided this was no time for a discussion about religion, so I turned to climb the stairs to our room.

"See you at supper, Lewis."

I remembered back to my early teen years when mother and dad had taken me to Sunday school, and my teacher had told the class that Jesus was born of a virgin girl named Mary. My college Bible professor had declared there was no such thing as miracles, only myths that had normal explanations incomprehensible many centuries ago. Professor Ruck also explained that the word "virgin" often meant "young woman." I had also learned in medical school embryology class that no female animal of any species could produce a male offspring without a male sexual partner. Such a thing would require a miracle, and miracles don't really happen.

During the course of the following week, I learned new and exciting things about the world of the operating room. I identified and classified the types and sizes of silk thread and catgut sutures, ranging from the strong, thick number 2 down to the hair-thin 000000, more readily known as 6-0. If they get any smaller than this, I thought, we'll need magnifying glasses to use them.

I learned that the "surgeon's knot" differs from the "granny knot;" the extra twist in the surgeon's knot prevents it from loosening while the second loop is made. I quickly became deft at tying by hand with thumb over finger, then finger over thumb. I also learned how to tie knots with instruments like needle holders and forceps, something that could be managed in spaces too small for hands and fingers.

Following elective surgery each day, I practiced backing through the swinging doors of the operating rooms, holding my scrubbed hands in front of myself, being careful not to touch anything. I also asked the circulating nurses to help me practice slipping into the surgical gowns, putting on rubber gloves, and maintaining surgical sterile technique. I prepared myself to assist on real, "live" operations when it was to become my turn the following week.

A few days later, having scrubbed in as second assistant on an appendectomy, a hernia repair, and knife wounds incurred in a lover's quarrel, I assisted the senior surgical resident, Amos Tutwiler. We were to remove two sebaceous cysts the size and shape of Georgia pecans from the back of a middle-age woman. The tumors were located directly under the edge of her bra straps and caused frequent irritation, even infection. Mrs. Jamison was somewhat drowsy as the result of pre-operative morphine she had received.

As Dr. Tutwiler injected novocaine around one of the cysts, the patient exclaimed, "Where do you get those dull needles, from some veterinarian's rejection pile?"

"I personally sharpened this needle," Amos replied, "and I only use it on special patients."

He whispered, "The discomfort comes mostly from the rapid distension of the tissues by the novocaine. If you inject slowly, it hurts much less."

Amos sliced the skin over the mound, taking care not to cut deep enough to open the wall of the cyst itself. Using blunt-nose scissors, he teased and snipped the tissue from the smooth mass that began to take on the appearance of a yellow bird egg.

"If you break the cyst wall, the junk will ooze out, and it will collapse, making complete removal much tougher," Amos explained. "Always handle with care to prevent rupture by sharp instruments or too much pulling or pushing."

Soon the cyst was excised, and Dr. Tutwiler cut the final strands of tissue that released it. Bleeding was minimal, and I was permitted to tie catgut loops around two small oozing blood vessels before Amos closed the incision itself with half a dozen black silk stitches spaced every quarter inch apart.

"You've seen one, now you can do the other one," he said.

Grady had long been known as a place where new doctors could often: See One, Do One, Teach One. Now I was to experience step two of this format.

Fresh drapes were arranged around the second cyst, and the two doctors exchanged places. Mrs. Jamison shifted her shoulders a bit, but seemed almost asleep. I took the scalpel with a curved number 15 blade and made a very shallow cut over the cyst to mark the line of my planned incision. The patient stiffened and let out a howl.

"Ouch! That hurts."

"It's okay, Mrs. Jamison," Amos said reassuringly, "we're just putting in more novocaine for the second cyst."

"You're still using that dull needle."

Amos casually handed the novocaine syringe to me. In my excitement, I had forgotten to inject the anesthetic around the second cyst and had sliced the patient's sensitive skin. I was glad Mrs. Jamison's face was turned away from me so she couldn't see the flush of red that suffused my neck and temples. After a couple of deep breaths, I gingerly injected the novocaine and successfully, if slowly, removed the second cyst in the same manner Amos had done with the first. I would long remember my initiation into surgery.

Every morning at eight o'clock, Lewis and I joined the two second year residents and the senior resident to accompany the professor of surgery or one of the several visiting staff surgeons. The visiting staff surgeons practiced in the city and volunteered on the teaching staff, on ward rounds in the half of the hospital that served the colored patients. Bill and Arnold made their rounds in the section for white patients. The interns would swap after the first two months.

Each new patient would be surrounded by a group of men in white coats. House staff wore short jackets; teachers wore long coats. One of the interns recited the history and physical findings, the results of laboratory tests, and X-rays, if any. The instructor would then examine the patient with his own stethoscope and flashlight. Lastly, after a question or two directed to the intern or resident, the professor discussed significant facts about the patient's condition and treatment plan. Patients who had already undergone surgery would be checked and their progress discussed. Occasionally the teacher would assign something for an intern to read about in a library text and asked to report back another day. Ward rounds were learning experience without equal.

On the female ward, the group approached one bed that at first glance appeared empty. It was my turn to tell about the diminutive, elderly woman who had been admitted late the previous afternoon with intermittent stomach pains and yellow tinted eyeballs. Detecting a slight bulge under the bed sheet, I handed the chart to Lewis and gently pulled the sheet down.

Annie Johnson opened her eyes and, recognizing my face, said, "Thank God it's you, doctor. I was so scared when I saw all those white coats that I thought you all was angels and I had died and gone to heaven."

"It's all right, Annie, these are all doctors who want to help you get well."

Annie's symptoms and tests all pointed to gallstones that were blocking her bile duct and damaging her liver. Bilirubin, a chemical produced in the liver from red blood cells which had died of old age after their normal life span of four months, should have drained from Annie's liver into her small intestine. Because stones were blocking the bile ducts, bilirubin had backed up into Annie's circulating blood and deposited its yellow color into her skin and eyeballs, where its presence was easily visible. Patients with jaundice are often morose and depressed, even as Shakespeare acknowledged in one of his plays, but Annie's optimistic nature had suffered no depression. She was scheduled for surgery the next day, and I was expected to scrub in as second assistant.

In the surgery changing room next morning, I was slipping on some old shoes when Pete Peterson, a second year surgery resident, came through the door in a slow shuffle. Pete was known to drink to excess on his nights off, and he appeared to be suffering from one of his frequent hangovers. I noticed that Pete's hands trembled slightly as he raised his cup of black coffee to his lips.

"I shouldn't have gone out to dinner with that old college buddy of mine who blew through town yesterday," he said. "I'll be okay, but my nerves are a bit tense this morning."

Pete and I had both completed our change of clothes and shoes when in bounded Dr. P. Claude Jackson, a member of the volunteer attending staff. A stiff collar and polka dot bow tie kept the senior physician's chin high and pointed directly forward. His greying brown hair was parted exactly in the midline and smoothed down on both sides. Small, round, rimless glasses sat upon his aquiline nose, under which a thin mustache spread to tiny waxed tips. Dr. Jackson's face made me think of an old daguerrotype picture of my own grandfather.

I thought, With the first name being Percival, its no wonder he prefers to be called P. Claude.

Pete rolled his eyes upward, let out a quiet, lengthy sigh and straightened his shoulders. Dr. Jackson had the reputation of being a stickler for small details that resulted in lengthening the time of cases he was involved with. His work was neat, but tedious—not exactly the type of situation Pete was in need of this day. He finished his coffee with a large gulp and set his mind to make the best of the coming trial.

When Dr. Jackson, Pete and I had finished scrubbing and had pushed our way through the operating room doors, the anesthetist was already inserting the eight-inch rubber tube between Annie's vocal cords and into her trachea. Through it she would pump in oxygen and ether to insure that the frail woman would breathe easily and smoothly and stay quietly asleep.

"You can prep now," she said to the circulating nurse.

When the scrub nurse assisted me in slipping on a pair of rubber gloves, I suddenly realized I had placed two fingers of my left hand into a single finger hole of the glove. Trying not to call attention to my predicament, I waited until the student nurse had tied the strings at the back of my surgical gown, then stretched the offending glove far enough to readjust my fingers into each intended slot. If I had only realized how often that happens to all surgeons, I would have laughed and calmly snapped the glove into place or asked the scrub nurse to pull the finger slot out to allow my fingers to separate and slide into the correct holes.

After the patient's belly had been washed and painted with an iodine antiseptic solution, cotton towels and sheets were draped over her body and extremities, leaving only an open rectangle below her right rib cage where the incision was planned. As Pete attached the sharp pointed towel clips to the corners of the towels framing the area, Dr. Jackson said sharply, "Wait a minute, doctor!"

Pete's hand jerked upward about six inches as he stiffened like a plucked banjo string.

"You've caught the patient's skin in that clip," Dr. Jackson said.

"Yes, sir," stammered Pete, "that keeps the towels from slipping."

"I don't like to poke unnecessary holes in the patient's skin," the senior man added. "Attach another clip to the big drape and that will hold it satisfactorily."

Pete finally secured the drapes in a manner that suited his instructor and prepared to make the initial incision. He had just touched the tip of the sharp blade to the dark skin when he was jerked to a rigid halt by another "Wait a minute, doctor!"

The Bard-Parker scalpel literally jumped out of Pete's hand and clattered to the floor. I wondered how much of this Pete's strained nerves could take. Dr. Jackson seemed to ignore the lost knife and said he wanted to rearrange the instruments on the Mayo stand that extended over the patient's chest area. Pete accepted another scalpel from the scrub nurse, who smiled gently behind her face mask, as I caught the twinkle in her pale blue eyes. After hesitating long enough to believe there would not be another explosive outburst from Dr. Jackson, Pete made a deep, reasonably straight cut through the black skin. From that point, things moved along quite well. Dr. Jackson, though somewhat picky, was competent and confident as he guided each step of the operation. Once he asked the anesthetist to increase the percentage of oxygen when Annie's blood looked a bit darker than he liked.

The gall bladder was found to be thick-walled and nearly full of rough, dark brown stones. Dr. Jackson showed Pete how to reattach the bile ducts and test their patency, then watched as Pete sewed the muscles and deep layers of flesh together. Dr. Jackson allowed me to insert the last five skin stitches as he and Pete discussed the post-operative care of the patient. I was surprised to realize how closely he was watching when Dr. Jackson once told me not to tie the silk sutures quite so tight and to replace the one I had just completed.

Later, as I changed out of the surgery clothes, I realized the enormity of what I had just participated in. Although I had witnessed a gall bladder operation, I knew I wasn't ready to try one on my own. This was serious surgery, not a simple removal of a skin cyst.

My thoughts drifted back to the freshman class in anatomy. Another student and I had dissected every organ, bone, numerous blood vessels and nerves in the inert body of an elderly Negro man whom no one had claimed for burial. Lying in a vat of formaldehyde every night, the stiff, shrunken body was brought out each morning and placed on a marble slab for the students. For that class of seventy students, thirty five such cadavers served as important tools of learning.

How different, yet familiar, the organs in a living body appeared to me versus the wrinkled, dry, pungent organs in the anatomy lab. I reflected on the marvels of the human body that worked in such a complex, yes almost miraculous way, converting a variety of foods into tiny particles of carbohydrates, proteins, and fatty acids that served as fuel for all the bodily functions. The more I learned in medical school, the more I realized how much more there was to be learned about the physiology of the body and what went wrong when it failed to work properly. It all seemed too complicated to be the result of chance and time, as those who taught Darwin's theory of evolution believed. I found myself posing more questions than answers as I continued to explore the marvels of the human body.

Every other Thursday afternoon, the four interns and two second year surgery residents were entertained by a visit from Dr. Beauregard Pollard, or "Polly" to his family and colleagues. His students used the nickname only out of earshot. Dr. Pollard enjoyed a busy practice in town, but, having inherited a sizeable fortune, chose the number of hours he would work. He often slipped away on short fishing trips whenever rumor reached him that the objects of his quest were biting with special frenzy at one of his favorite haunts in South Georgia or North Florida.

The second year men knew the proctologist was approaching; they smelled the smoke of the heavy, dark cigar that perennially protruded from his mouth. Polly puffed the stogies as he lectured, and even clenched one between his teeth in the outpatient surgery room, where it was strictly forbidden by the hospital; it was said he laid them aside only to eat or sleep. A plump, jovial, bald-headed, cherubic-faced character, Dr. Pollard enjoyed sprinkling down-to-earth wisdom with his medical acumen. He faced a semicircle of his six "scrubs" and blew an enormous cloud of smoke toward the ceiling.

"Who is Andrew H. Brown?" he asked, pointing his cigar toward Arnold Burnside.

Arnold, searching his memory for the identity of some prominent doctor, politician, author, or local citizen, stammered, "Uhh, uhh, I don't know, sir."

Being seated at the far end of the line, I had time to think as each of the young doctors in turn stumbled with the answer. Just before it was my turn, I remembered.

"Andrew H. Brown is the Andy of *The Amos and Andy Show*," I said.

"That's right," Dr. Pollard replied. "Now Andy is a great philosopher, and he says there are two things you can't escape: death and taxes. But he also said something that applies to your patients after you've operated on them for hemorrhoids: 'Never send a boy to do a man's job.'"

I wondered if Andy had ever said such a thing, but these types of quotes often enlivened the good doctor's lectures.

"After a hemorrhoid operation, your patient will have a lot of pain, so don't prescribe two aspirin or a B. C. powder. Give them a good slug of morphine or dilaudid and you'll make a lot of satisfied and loyal followers," Dr. Pollard emphasized.

Two patients were lying nearby, awaiting proctoscopic examinations. Dr. Pollard hung his coat and vest in the lecture room, rolled up the sleeves of his white shirt, and sat on the stool facing the bare behind of a rather obese woman who was lying on her side on the examination table. A nurse had cleansed and draped the large buttocks and anal region.

"Hold her upper leg skyward," he said as he generously greased the end of the long metal tube call a proctoscope.

"I wear these darned gloves to keep my hands clean," he added.

In spite of his usually casual demeanor, Dr. Pollard was gentle and deft in his handling of patients. With a continual flow of comforting remarks to the obviously tense woman, he inserted the pipe into her rectum and peered through his bifocals at the walls of the convoluted, pinkish canal.

"Ah, there's the little beggar, " he said. "You boys take a look at that polyp on the right side just beyond the end of this scope."

His words were slightly slurred as he spoke through clenched teeth, not being able to remove his cigar with his gloved, greasy hands.

One by one the students looked through the proctoscope.

"Hurry up, Doc," the patient moaned, "that thing hurts. Do all of them have to have a look?"

"It's all right, honey, we're almost finished."

Reaching for the cautery that the nurse offered, Dr. Pollard, having already injected novocaine around the reddish, mushroom-shaped tumor that protruded into the colon and had caused intermittent bleeding, burned the offending lesion into charred fragments and blew the cautery smoke away with a puff of his own cigar smoke. Once more, each of the interns viewed the results before the instrument was removed and the woman allowed to relax.

After the second case, an anal fissure that required a light touch of the cautery and medication, Dr. Pollard retrieved his vest, coat, and hat.

"I give you this warning myself. It is not from Mr. Brown. Just remember you can't screw all the women in the world who want to be screwed, and you can't drink all the whiskey in the world, so don't try either."

With an extra large puff on his diminishing cigar, he added, "See you in a couple of weeks, fellows. Give that lady a prescription for six quarter grain morphines."

AUGUST 1945

Dear Mom and Dad,

Well, things are rolling along pretty fast here at "The Gradies." I'm learning how to go to sleep real quick any time of the day or night when I get the chance. There's so much night work that the only way I can get enough "shut eye" is to grab a nap or two every day for as little as fifteen minutes. I lie on my back with my arms folded across my chest, and I'm asleep as soon as I look at the insides of my eyelids. Arnold says all I need is a lily in my hands to be a perfect ad for a funeral home.

The food is pretty good, too. You know how I like breakfast. We have grits every other morning, pancakes about twice a week, and scrambled eggs nearly every day. One of the senior residents said the delicious biscuits are the specialty of one of the cooks whose name is—if you can believe it—"Pink Rose."

I don't think I've gained or lost a pound, but I haven't stepped on a scale to find out.

The medical service got a new chief last week. His name is Bert Duval, and he came from Boston. I haven't heard him talk yet, but others say he has a strong Yankee accent. You're gonna love this: Bert came by train and arrived in Atlanta after dark last Saturday night. Hailing a taxi at the Central Station, he asked to be taken to Grady Hospital. The driver figured that only the emergency rooms would be open late at night, so he took Bert to the colored Emergency Room entrance and let him out.

Two drunks were sleeping on the visitor benches, and there was no nurse at the desk. She had gone to the powder room while activity was at a low ebb. Bert heard a man howling like a hound dog at a full moon, as well as a male voice crooning Deep Purple from the same location. The noise was coming from behind the big curtain that separates the examining and minor operating table from the rest of the area. Dr. Duval peered around the curtain and saw Dr. Amos Tutwiler calmly sewing a bloody cut on the forehead of a really big black man. Amos would interrupt his singing long enough to shout, "Just hold still, Edgar, I'll be finished in a few minutes."

Edgar was yelling and moaning and thrashing his feet, but his head remained as still as a stone statue, yet no one was holding him down.

Dr. Duval introduced himself.

"As soon as I take a few more stitches, I'll walk you over to the living quarters," Amos told the newly arrived chief.

Bert couldn't understand why the injured man wasn't moving his head, but as he looked closer he discovered the answer. Amos had taken a stitch with heavy black silk thread through each of the drunk's ear lobes and tied them to the edge of the table. The guy couldn't roll or lift his head without tearing his ear lobes off. His hands were in the regular leather table side restraints, but his feet were free to kick, and his mouth could shout complaint. I think Bert came close to recalling the taxi and hot-footing it back to Boston. He did refuse Amos' invitation for a late night snack in the doctor's dining room.

I'm still enjoying the surgery service. There's so much work to be done and so few doctors to do it that I've already assisted on several operations and done a few minor procedures myself. You know how the war has taken so many physicians away from hospitals and practices.

The other day I told a patient he'd need minor surgery the next day. He said, "Doctor, it might be minor to you, but when it's done to me, I call it major."

I hope you are both well.

Love,

Curtis, Jr.

As I entered the doctor's dining room one hot Tuesday afternoon I noticed that Bill Andrews was signaling to me.

"When you get your tray, come on over. I've got some news for you."

I approached with a plate full of grits, eggs, bacon, toast, and a glass of milk. I seldom drank coffee, in spite of the long hours of work.

"It's a treat to have bacon. The dietician must have some pull with the rationing board," I said, as I slid into a chair next to my roommate.

Bill lowered his voice, leaned closer and whispered, "A friend of mine has offered me his car this Saturday night. I've got a date with that good-looking nurse, Nancy Rutherford. I hear she'll neck real good. Get yourself a date, and we'll go out to the Phi Chi house for some fun."

"But I haven't met any of the nurses yet. I don't know whom to ask."

"If you can't come up with someone by Friday, I'll ask Nancy to get a blind date for you."

"Okay, I'll see what I can do."

It was my turn to do rounds with the residents and the visiting surgeon. My patient, Annie, had recovered sufficiently from her gall bladder operation and had gone home. I had enjoyed stopping by her bed for a friendly visit each day while she was there. She had been born on a farm not far from Albany, though she called it "All-benny" like most of the residents of South Georgia. Annie had given birth to seven children, but only five reached adulthood. She now lived in Atlanta with a son who was a Baptist preacher. Annie talked with me about her faith in God, but I had only listened politely and responded with neutral comments.

"I never learned to read, doctor, but my preacher son reads Scripture to me every evening at home. Do you read the Bible each day, doctor?" Annie asked.

"I don't get much time to read anything except my medical books," I replied.

"There are so many comforting things in the Good Book that God wants us all to know, doctor. I'll pray that you have time to read it."

"Thank you, Annie."

I figured that prayer only made sense if there is a God who can hear human utterances and who can and will respond. But how is it possible for God to listen to prayers in many different languages and locations at the same time? That didn't make sense to me, but I was certain that Annie really believed prayer was genuine communication.

"I've got to get outta this hospital," Annie said, "so's I can help baby sittin' with those granchillun of mine."

I figured Annie would have some new stories to tell the grandkids about her adventure at the hospital.

Boredom never figured into an intern's life, and this day was no different. I had kept busy with admissions, paper work, physical exams, discussions with the chief resident, and one hour in the medical library to research surgery on stomach and duodenal ulcers. My own father had been operated on for an ulcer several years earlier. When mild abdominal pains developed some ten years later, he checked into Johns Hopkins Hospital in Baltimore for a thorough evaluation. After a physical exam and a psychiatric workup, he was told it was anxiety or nervous tension. Unhappy with the assessment, Dad insisted that his pain was real, left Baltimore and returned to Atlanta, where he found a surgeon who would do exploratory surgery. Old adhesions from the prior operation were found and loosened. My father had been fine since then.

I was to assist on an operation called a gastrojejunostomy—the word rolled around in my mouth like an all day sucker—so now I would see what my father had endured. The surgeon would make a hole in the bottom of the stomach and a matching hole in the segment of the small intestine called the jejunum, curving immediately below the stomach. By sewing the two holes together, a passage would be made that allowed food to be shunted away from the ulcer that had eroded a raw pit where the stomach and the duodenum meet. As a result, the ulcer should heal.

During the three hour surgery, Lewis and I took turns as second and first assistant to Amos Tutwiler. Amos was a thorough and patient teacher, and I gained valuable experience clamping and tying bleeding vessels, seeing exactly how the upper abdominal viscera connected to each other as well as the vital liver and pancreas. I gently handled the sinuous small intestine, learned the intricate way the nearly transparent mesentery encased the organs, and realized more clearly how a surgeon has to be aware of more than just the immediate area of cutting and sewing. I found myself watching the arterial pulsations, the color of the oozing venous blood, the routes of important nerves and vessels, all a symphony of homeostasis necessary for the survival of the marvelous creation called the human body. I was thrilled to be a part of a profession involved in healing.

Long after supper, I made my way to the surgery ward for a final check on the post-op patient. Lifting the chart from the nurses' desk, I studied the pages while walking into the spacious ward. The quiet was broken only by snores from the sleeping patients. As I rounded the corner of the first cubicle with its drapes shut, my peripheral vision registered the movement of a bulky form moving toward me. I tried to sidestep the inevitable collision, but couldn't avoid a glancing crash into the strange object. A feminine voice emitted a high pitched, "Oh, no. Oh, NOOO!" as a stack of four enameled bed pans cascaded to the hard floor and bounced explosively in different directions. The sudden, intense noise jarred every ear in the ward. Urine sprayed around the room, soaking my trouser legs, socks and shoes. Bed curtains flew open, and those patients who were able, sat up to see what the sudden commotion was all about.

The person holding the stack of bed pans, now spilled hither and yon, was a wide-eyed and petite student nurse, clad in the blue and white uniform assigned to nurses-in-training. She appeared to be just over five feet tall and probably weighed no more than a hundred pounds. Her white student cap sat atop the most beautiful wave of red hair that I had ever seen. The girl's white cheeks quickly assumed their own reddish hue that crept from her collar to her temples.

"I'm so sorry. I was looking at this chart and didn't see you in time."

"I couldn't see you through this—aah—that stack of bedpans," the girl replied.

As she surveyed the mess spreading across the floor, she sighed, "Golly gee, I'll be all night cleaning up this mess."

"Thank goodness none of that was being collected for the lab or volume reports," she added.

"The least I can do is help you clean it up," I said, still gazing at the shiny red hair.

"What's your name?"

"Betty Jo Chandler, with no "e" on the Jo," she said, pointing to the name tag pinned above her left breast. The white apron covering her blue uniform was cinched tight around her waist and curved upward over her small, but well defined bust, and encircled her neck.

The name etched on the rectangular plastic pin verified her statement.

"Where do they keep the floor mop?"

"In a closet at the far end of the room. I'll get it," she said. Turning to the patients, she added, "You can all go back to sleep. The building isn't falling down."

I gathered the scattered bedpans and rinsed them in a sink designed for that purpose in a small room opposite the nurses' desk. Betty Jo retrieved the mop from the janitor's closet, and we both began a silent clean up.

After several awkward minutes, I said, "I'm very sorry to have caused you so much trouble. Would you consider letting me make it up to you on a date this Saturday night?"

"I ought never to speak to you again," Betty Jo replied. "In fact, I don't know why I'm speaking to you now, except that I haven't been out of this slave labor camp since I arrived here six weeks ago, and I'm getting cabin fever. What time Saturday night?"

"My roommate, Bill Andrews, has access to a car. He has a date with Nancy Rutherford. Bill said if I could get a date, we'd go to the Phi Chi fraternity house, play some records, dance, and have a few drinks. By the way, what do you drink, or do you drink?"

"I might have a glass or two of Scotch and soda, but I don't drink much, so don't get any wrong ideas," Betty Jo said sharply.

I had studied the girl's face from several angles as we worked with mops and paper towels, soaking up the pungent urine from the linoleum floor. She was more cute than beautiful. Her thin, arched eyebrows appeared dark red. Her light brown eyes flashed under abundant, long lashes. Her nose was neither pointed not upturned, just average, lips were full, with a tiny dimple at each corner. Her teeth were small, very white and straight, and the little chin was smooth and rounded. Altogether a better than average looker, I concluded.

"I'd better let you get back to your work. Thanks for saying you'll go out with me. We'll pick you and Nancy up at the nurses' building about seven thirty Saturday."

Bill, Lewis, Arnold and I were hunched over lunch on Friday when Will McMath, chief resident in the Eye, Ear, Nose and Throat Department, interrupted our conversation.

"I'm doing an elective tracheotomy at one thirty," he said. "It's an operation you may have to do in a hurry some day, so this would be a good chance for you to learn it when you're not under pressure. Meet me in the white operating room in one hour."

Pointing an empty fork toward me, Bill asked, "Did you get a date for tomorrow night?"

"Yes, Betty Jo Chandler."

"Don't know her," Bill said. "How'd you meet her?"

"I'll tell you the story later, but it involves a stack of bedpans."

"Sounds romantic. Oh well, let's check what the surgery books say about tracheotomies and get ready for Dr. McMath's case. I'd like to see one before I have to do one," Bill concluded.

"You guys tell me about it tonight," Arnold said, as he reached for the last chocolate chip cookie on the dessert plate. "I have to help Amos Tutwiler in the colored O. R. this afternoon."

In the changing room, Will McMath explained the procedure we were about to witness.

"Most of the tracheotomies you'll have to do will be on children with croup or diphtheria. We get a few adults with throat injuries or laryngeal edema. This man today needs one due to a lung condition. He needs suctioning of his trachea and bronchi every few hours, and a tracheotomy will make it much easier for the nurses to do that."

Will McMath, raised in Waycross, Georgia, planned to return to his hometown when he completed his residency the following June. He was a quiet, studious type, working extremely hard to handle all the work that was formerly divided between two residents in peace time. Private practice would seem slow compared to his frantic pace at "The Gradies."

As the four doctors gathered around the operating table, the moist rattling sound coming from the patient's chest was apparent. The man was barely conscious and offered only weak groans as Will injected novocaine into the skin of his neck, just above the upper notch of the sternum.

"In emergency situations, you may not have time or need for novocaine," he said. "First, feel for the trachea as low as you can. You must not cut into the larynx, where the vocal cords are located. You can see this man's Adam's apple, and you must stay below it, but little kids don't have one, so you just have to stay as low in the neck as possible with them."

Will spread his thumb and index finger gently from the center line of the patient's neck toward each side, making the cartilage rings of the trachea appear as faint ridges under the taut skin.

"If you cut exactly in the midline, there's not much bleeding," Will said. "And make your first cut deep enough to get right down to the windpipe. If it's an emergency, you don't want to get lost fishing around in the soft tissues of the neck. Don't forget, the thyroid gland wraps around the trachea low down, but it's quite thin and narrow in the midline. Even if you do slice into the gland, that won't hurt a thing."

Using his two fingers again to spread the vertically aligned incision apart, Will exposed the trachea and its rings. With a few more deft slices of the knife, he spread the tissues with a small hemostat and reached his target.

"Have your trach tube ready," Will said. "There's a set of all sizes in every tracheotomy kit in both emergency rooms and in the O. R.'s. This guy will take a size five. Curtis, you remove the inner tube and stick that little guide in the outer tube, please."

I located the size five curved silver tube with its side wings and its inner tube held in place by a rotating key. Loosening the lock, I removed the inner cannula and inserted the curved plunger guide snugly until the solid, olive-shaped tip protruded slightly from the lower end.

"Now attach a strip of that ribbon tape on both wings so we can tie it around his neck after I get the tube in place. We don't want him coughing it out right away," Will added, as he sliced through one of the tracheal cartilage rings.

Air whistled through the slit as the patient breathed in and out. Will slipped the tip of the silver tube through the newly made hole, curved it downward until the wings of the tube rested flat against the skin, then removed the guide. He eased a gauze pad under the wings of the tube and taped it to the skin that the nurse had just painted with benzoin to increase the stickiness of the adhesive. The two ribbons of cotton tape that I had tied to the wings were of unequal lengths, one short and one long. Will slipped the long piece under the patient's neck and tied it to the shorter piece on the side of the neck.

"Use a good square knot," he said. "We don't want it to come loose and have the tube fly across the room when he coughs."

Inserting a long rubber catheter through the tracheotomy tube, Dr. McMath suctioned the sticky mucus from the entire trachea and some of the larger bronchial branches. The patient's breathing was immediately quieter and less labored. Will then inserted and locked the inner tube inside the outer tube.

"The purpose of this inner cannula is so you can take it out and clean it when phlegm dries and clogs the tube from time to time. The outer tube stays in place." After thanking McMath for the lesson, we interns changed back into our whites.

"You know," Bill remarked, "it's a lot more real seeing a procedure than just reading about it." We all agreed.

"By the way, Curtis," Bill said, "do you have your booze for tomorrow night?"

"Yeah, I bought one pint of Scotch whiskey with last month's pay check."

"Now tell me how you met this nurse you've conned into a date."

"Well, it was sorta like a story Uncle Remus might tell. . . ."

Windows were wide open in the Phi Chi fraternity house that hot Saturday night as Bill drove the aging Plymouth sedan into the parking lot behind the two story frame building. The foursome mounted the three stairs onto the side porch that served as the usual entrance into the house. Sounds of Artie Shaw's big band rendition of Begin the Beguine vibrated through the screen door. Three couples were dancing in the large, oak-floored living room. The new arrivals dodged the dancers and went through the dining room into the kitchen. Someone had provided a large bag of crushed ice, a few bottles of soda, and orange and grape pop. Bill eyed the grape soda and said, "We used to make ethyl alcohol in chemistry lab, add it to grape juice, and call it "Purple Passion." It didn't taste as smooth as vodka, but it was pretty powerful."

Bill lifted a bottle of Four Roses from his brown paper bag and poured some into two glasses. Holding them at eye level, he judged the amount like a student in chemistry lab.

"Is that stuff rationed?" Nancy asked.

"Oh, sorry," Bill replied. "Just a habit of mine."

I opened the bottle of Johnnie Walker Red and mixed it with bubbling soda water, before handing it over to Betty Jo. The foursome clinked their glasses all around before sipping the contents.

Hearing the melodious strains of Marie played by the Tommy Dorsey orchestra, Betty Jo said, "That's one of my favorites. Let's dance."

I had danced just enough in college to do the basic box step or fox trot, and even a little jitterbug, but I was overly conscious of my feet and had difficulty concentrating on the conversation. Betty Jo, on the other hand, was a smooth dancer and moved with ease. I struggled to bend my six foot frame down to my much shorter partner when we decided on a slow dance.

The only light in the room came from two floor lamps. The dim rays occasionally reflected off Betty Jo's shiny red hair that felt soft and smooth to my cheek. The faint fragrance of perfume served as an additional delight, and I danced in a daze for several minutes. It was a few seconds after the music stopped before I became aware of it.

Someone began to put on another record when Betty Jo looked up and said, "I haven't thanked you for helping me clean up that mess of urine the other night, you clumsy goat."

Reaching both arms around my neck, she raised herself onto her toes and planted a long, moist kiss squarely on my lips. My surprise was overcome by a quick response. Encircling Betty Jo's tiny torso with both arms, I pulled her close and returned the kiss with an equally satisfying one.

"You're quite welcome," I said, as I led my companion to the table where we had left our drinks and then to a leather sofa, while my pulse resumed its normal rate.

My thoughts went back to a student nurse named Lillian whom I had dated during my senior year in med school. Being the studious type, I had dated very little in college and the first three years of medical school. I had attended parties, shows, and dances with Lillian on several occasions, but had never kissed her until one night when we arrived at her dormitory at the end of a date. We sat quietly in the car, and Lillian had made no move to open the door on her side. She turned her face toward me as I leaned over, bringing my lips close to hers. Lillian must have never been kissed, and the result was the greatest disappointment I could ever remember. There was no response on her part, and I felt I might as well have put my lips to a dead fish. It was the last time I ever saw Lillian.

I wrapped my arm around Betty Jo's shoulders, brought her closer and resumed the delicious kissing she had begun on the dance floor. This, I quickly realized, was an incredibly wonderful activity.

Bill and Nancy were dancing slowly to the strains of Stardust, a popular song from the pen of Hoagy Carmichael. Anyone could see why Bill was so jazzed about Nancy. The girl had the face and figure of a Petty drawing from an Esquire magazine. No wonder she was the most popular date out of all the student nurses. Her medium brown, slightly wavy shoulder length hair framed a superbly beautiful face. Nancy's one hundred and thirty pounds were distributed in an hour glass shape of 36 - 26 - 36 inch measurements. On a hospital chart she would have been clinically described as a "well developed, well nourished, young adult female." How much more exciting it was to visually round out the details of such a sterile description. Bill and Nancy moved towards another sofa and entwined their arms around each other.

Betty Jo was no novice at the art of kissing, and the two of us thoroughly enjoyed getting to know each other better.

The evening passed too quickly, but it was a much needed change from the intense pressure that interns and nurses face each day.

Bill drove the quartet back to the nurses' dormitory before the 11:30 curfew time, let the girls out, and parked the borrowed car in the tiny lot behind the hospital.

"Thanks for the invitation, Bill, It was a great evening. I hope we get to do it again."

"Wipe the lipstick off your mouth, Curtis," Bill replied. "You look like a little boy caught in a watermelon patch."

SEPTEMBER, 1945

Dear Mom and Dad,

Now that the war is over, you won't have to worry about me getting killed by some Japanese aviator who wants to hurry to his great geisha house in the sky by a suicide attack on a field hospital - a place I might have been sent after my internship is finished next June. I'd like to stay here at Grady for specialty training if possible. We'll see what happens next summer.

I thought you both would get a kick out of something that happened over at Piedmont Hospital a couple months ago. Dr. Tutwiler's cousin is on staff there, and he told Amos about it.

It seems that a very sick woman was brought into the emergency room one evening in a semi-comatose condition, her blood pressure off the top of the scale, and her kidneys in failure. She was accompanied by what seemed a remarkably large family, most of them middle aged adults, who were somewhat shabbily dressed. Their olive-toned skin and dark hair was a contrast to the typical Atlanta resident. One of the people had somehow heard of Dr. Clinton Durwood and specifically requested that he handle her case. Even though the hour was late, the family insisted that Durwood tend to her.

Dr. Durwood, who lives close to the hospital, was called by the admissions nurse. She explained that the case couldn't wait until morning. Clinton had just finished dinner, so he slipped on his tie and coat and went to the hospital. He could hardly get into her room because of the pressing crowd of visitors, no fewer than a dozen of them. It was explained to Dr. Durwood that his patient was actually a gypsy queen, and that she had not yet named a successor to her throne. The important members of her tribe were sticking as close to her as fleas on a yard dog because someone had to be present when this vital information was passed on.

Clinton was able to clear the room of most of the tribe members, whereupon they merely shifted to other areas of the hospital and settled in. They filled the waiting room, the lobby, the lounges, and some even slipped into the doctor's dressing room. Dr. Durwood allowed a man he thought to be her husband stay in the room. When Clinton sent the nurse for an ophthalmoscope, the man edged right up to the doctor's face, brandished a switch-blade knife under his chin, and said, "You're not going to let her die, are you, Doctor? If she dies, I'm holding you responsible."

Clinton was scared speechless, so he pretended to do some more examining before opening his mouth.

"Don't worry. We'll take good care of her. Please stand back and give me some room."

By then the nurse had returned. She didn't notice the slight pallor on Dr. Durwood's face. Clinton used the ophthalmoscope and noted the changes in the retinal arteries that confirmed the seriousness of the hypertension. He gave instructions for medications and started to leave. The fierce looking man stopped him just outside the door and repeated his admonition about not letting the queen die, and what would happen if she did. Dr. Durwood hurried home, but he didn't sleep well that night.

The doctor cautiously made his rounds twice each day, each time keeping a wary eye on the gypsy consort, hoping not to encounter the knife again. He was happy that the blood pressure medications and the diuretics were working. For two more days, the woman clung to life, and even improved a bit.

A considerable number of gypsies set up housekeeping in the hospital, eating meals in hallways and other public rooms. The administrator had a dickens of a time trying to get them out. They would leave, but sneak back in the night to sleep wherever they could find a quiet place.

Dr. Durwood was too scared to call the police about the knife threats, but he tried to think of a solution to his dilemma. Finally he hit upon a brilliant idea. He spoke to the prince in the hall and said, "Your queen needs a very special treatment. I've contacted the best doctor in the country for this condition, and he's willing to treat her."

As the prince began to finger his knife again, Dr. Durwood continued.

"I've arranged for a charter flight on Eastern Airlines to take her and several of her relatives to New York this afternoon. One of our best house doctors will fly right along with her to see that nothing goes wrong."

"Nothing had better go wrong," was the gruff reply.

An ambulance, followed by an old, rusty station wagon packed with gypsies, took the queen, the consort, an intern, and one nurse to the Atlanta airport to board the plane. After the plane was airborne, the prince moved to a seat near the intern, a tall, dark, handsome young man from a South American nation. When they were over North Carolina, the prince flashed his knife in the intern's face and said, "You won't let her die, will you, Doctor? If you do . . ."

The big Latin intern stared straight into the shorter man's eyes and calmly and clearly said, "Go back to your seat, you little bastard. If that woman dies, I'll be the first one to know, and the first thing I'm going to do is pick you up and throw your butt out that side door."

There was no further trouble, and the woman was safely put in an ambulance in New York and whisked away to the big teaching hospital. The intern received a handsome reward when he returned. The hospital never collected a penny of its bill, but Eastern Airlines was paid. They had insisted on cash before take-off.

Dr. Durwood had been afraid to ask for any money, so he never got paid. He says, however, that the fun of telling *the story is a fair exchange for the pay. And it's the kind of tale that gets more embellished each time it's told, especially the size of the knife.*

This hospital certainly stays busy. I seldom get a whole night's sleep, but I catch enough naps here and there to get by okay. I'm learning lots, and the chief residents say my work is pretty good. I have been out on a couple of dates with a cute little nurse. Nothing serious, but it is fun.

Love to you all,
Curtis, Jr.

"Hey, Curtis, I hear you're working in the emergency room this month," Arnold said as he seated himself at the dining room table with his plate of scrambled eggs and pancakes.

"Yeah, I go there after rounds on the surgical wards and whatever assisting I'm doing on the operating schedule each weekday morning."

"What about nights and weekends?" Arnold asked.

"Every other night and every Saturday, day and night this month."

"I start that schedule next month," Arnold said. "Did yours start last night?"

"Yes, and I learned a new trick."

"What was that?"

"A man came in about eight o'clock, holding a hand over his left ear and dancing like a Hindu on a bed of hot coals. He said a Japanese beetle, one of those little, hard back bugs that are common this time of year, had flown right into his ear canal and was clawing to get out. I got an ear speculum and a headlight and tried to grasp the thing with forceps. The guy wouldn't hold still, and the bug was wedged in so tight that I couldn't get a grip on it."

"So, what did you do?"

"Well the nurse who's worked in the E.R since Sherman came through Atlanta stopped me and said, "Doctor, fill his ear with mineral oil and drown the bug; then you can get it out easier.' It worked so slick. The bug stopped moving, and I used a tiny hook to slip it out backwards."

Saturday night came around soon enough. I watched the assistant resident, Dr. Frank Foote, handle a number of drunks, one broken wrist, an assortment of stomach aches, runny noses, coughs, fevers, and lacerations.

"Saturday nights are usually busy," Dr. Foote said. "You may have to handle a number of things yourself if I get tied up, but I'll help you if you get in over your head."

Dr. Foote was right. The patients kept coming, but not by themselves. So many family members, friends, and assorted onlookers drifted in that all the bench seats in the waiting room were taken. Noise and confusion permeated the halls. One of the two nurses was so busy managing the crowd in front of her desk that she couldn't help with the actual patients. Dr. Foote saw her frustration and whispered, "Let me clear this waiting room so you can help Dr. Benton with that arm laceration in section two."

Frank stood in the middle of the crowded reception area and said in a loud voice, "Miss Avondale, the patient in section two needs a blood transfusion. I'm going to the blood bank for some bottles. I want you to get everybody in this room ready to give blood as soon as I get back."

Dr. Foote had barely disappeared down the corridor when the room vacated, almost as if a giant vacuum had sucked them out.

"Works every time," Frank said as he returned with an armful of empty bottles and rubber tubing.

"I'm going to supper, Curtis," Frank called over his shoulder as he walked to the entrance of the tunnel that connected the two hospitals.

I had just finished sewing a cut on a young man's arm and was helping the nurse put a clean sheet on the exam table when the swinging double doors of the ambulance entrance burst open.

"Quick, doctor, this child is dying," shouted a policeman, as he carried a young girl about four years old in his outstretched arms.

The child was gasping for breath through blue lips. Almost no air reached the tiny lungs as the sternum and rib cage collapsed inward with each intense effort of inspiration. With head rolled backward and eyes closed, the girl was clinging desperately to what little life remained in her.

I quickly shined my penlight into the tiny throat. Covering the swollen tonsils was a dirty gray film.

Diphtheria, I thought to myself.

Nurse Beck also recognized the problem and was already moving toward the instrument cabinet as I yelled, "Get the tracheotomy set and call Dr. Foote."

Nurse Beck unrolled the sterile contents onto a nearby Mayo stand and said, "Dr. Foote can't possibly get here in time; you'll have to do it yourself, and quick."

This was a true medical emergency. Inaction meant certain and quick death. Inappropriate action could lead to the same result. Rapidly wiping iodine solution on the little girl's neck from chin to breastbone, I slipped on a pair of sterile gloves, put my thoughts into gear, scrolling up the list of steps for tracheotomy in rapid order, rather like an open textbook coming into focus in a vivid dream - extend the head backward, place a rolled towel under the neck, push the tissues away from the midline with thumb and forefinger, cut low in the neck, cut deep enough on the first slice, spread the tissues with a hemostat to minimize bleeding, find the tracheal rings, cut through one cartilage into the airway, and, especially, be quick about it! My silent prayer was, "God, please let me find that trachea in time." That prayer must have been a reflex from my childhood days, for I had rejected the practice of prayer several years ago in college.

With the child already unconscious, there was no need or time to inject a local anesthetic. Rapidly and smoothly the scalpel blade cut the dusky brown skin in a one inch long vertical straight line. What little blood seeped from the fresh wound was a dark red, almost purple. The child was still making feeble efforts to breathe, but no air was reaching the oxygen-starved lungs. My own pulse sounded in my ears like the ticking of a bomb. How many seconds, I wondered, remained on the clock of this little girl's life? Was it mere coincidence that I had witnessed a tracheotomy less than a month ago? Those long hours at the dissection table in first year anatomy class had given me the confidence to recognize vital body parts in the patient's neck.

The closed tips of the hemostat encountered the resistance of cartilage, and I spread the serrated jaws apart to reveal the whitish ring of the "C" shaped structure. A quick vertical cut through the firm cartilage and a twist of the scalpel to a horizontal position opened a hole about the size of a soda straw, small by comparison to an entire trachea, but large enough for life-giving air to whistle through as the child made one more effort to inhale. Within seconds the precious oxygen found its way into the blood capillaries of the lung's air sacs, and then on to the inert brain.

I thought, What a marvelous organ is the heart, which keeps beating for a while after the lungs cease to function.

Another successful breath followed, then a third, and the girl's body relaxed as she began to breathe easily. Exhaustion had taken her to the brink of death, but life was rapidly returning. I remembered that a brain without oxygen for longer than six minutes might suffer permanent damage, and after ten minutes it definitely does.

Nurse Beck glanced at her watch. "Three and a half minutes, Dr. Benton. I felt like I was holding my breath the entire time."

The little girl's skin resumed its chocolate brown color, and the little blood in the surgical wound became a brighter red. As Dr. Foote rushed into the room, he made a quick assessment of the situation.

"Use a number one tube," he said. "Good job, Curtis. When did you learn to do a tracheotomy?"

"Recently," I replied, trying to keep my voice steady.

After securing the tracheotomy tube in the child's neck, I stripped off my gloves and noticed that my hands were trembling slightly. Wiping the sweat from my brow and neck, I sat down while Nurse Beck prepared the diphtheria antitoxin and shared the good news with the girl's two parents, whom everyone had nearly forgotten under the pressure of the moment.

I thought of how often ordinary humans perform extraordinary feats in emergencies, only to tremble and wonder how it was possible when the crisis was over. I then remembered that Annie Johnson had offered to pray for me regularly after she went home. The expression that "there are no atheists in foxholes" also flashed through my mind.

I had successfully made it through my first trial-by-fire. Once again I was aware of the thin margin between life and death. If I had not learned how to do a tracheotomy a few days earlier, I would probably have failed to save the little girl's life, and Dr. Foote would have arrived too late.

Maybe there is a God who cares about human beings, and maybe He hears and answers prayers. How would I have felt if I had failed? I wondered. Thinking of it as a chance or just being in the right place at the right time seemed like an unsatisfactory explanation at that moment.

The child's mother said, "How can we ever thank you, Doctor, for saving our Kendra's life? We will certainly keep you in our prayers. God bless you."

As I stood in the elevator before rounds the next morning, I was still trying to grasp the fact that I had actually saved a precious human life. The concept of human life as "precious" didn't fit with the concept of Darwinian evolution that I had studied in college. If human beings developed from apes by random mutation, and apes from lesser primates, and on down the evolutionary ladder to single-cell forms of life, where did concepts like "precious," "virtuous," "honorable," and so forth come from? On the other extreme, what was "precious" about Hitler, Stalin, or Tojo? It seemed to me that humans are qualitatively different from all other animals.

My attention was suddenly jerked back to the present as Professor of Surgery, Dr. Elkhart, and a quartet of surgery residents also stepped into the ancient elevator. Wondering what had occasioned such an early visit by the professor, I eased into a back corner and decided to follow the group. As the elevator rumbled to a pause on the second floor level, a large black woman, wrapped in a skimpy hospital gown, stepped aboard. A wide grin broke across her face as she clutched the free edge of the white garment that lacked a few inches of covering her very sizeable buttocks. As she shuffled sideways against the side wall of the elevator, Dr. Elkhart stared at the brilliant glow between the woman's thick lips. The four upper incisor teeth, completely capped with gold, sparkled as though emitting a light of their own. This was further enhanced by two rubies mounted on her teeth, as well as two brilliant diamonds, reflecting a rainbow of colors.

Dr. Elkhart stammered, "Good morning."

"Good morning, Doctors," came the cheery reply, the treasure chest of jewels, gold, and pearly teeth flashing brightly.

As the door rattled open on floor three, the patient side stepped her way out of the elevator and backed around the corner, careful to prevent exposure of her backside to the view of six male strangers.

Dr. Elkhart motioned Chief Resident Amos Tutwiler aside.

"You know, Doctor, we're due to present a couple of interesting cases at the American College of Surgeons meeting in the auditorium this afternoon," he said.

"Yes, Sir."

"That woman with the gold teeth . . . ," the professor said, "I don't care what she's in the hospital for, but have her at the conference at three o'clock. None of those Yankee surgeons attending the program has ever seen anything like that before."

Overhearing the plans, I realized that today's medical meeting would be anything but dull if Dr. Elkhart's little scheme was successful.

I climbed the stairs to the male surgical ward, and as I passed the nurses' desk, I noticed an obviously agitated patient, an equally upset orderly, and a bewildered nurse. A glance at the patient's chart revealed that he was scheduled for repair of an inguinal hernia that had been operated on three months before, but had developed a small gaping of the wound.

"What's the matter, John?" I inquired.

"This here fellow came at me with a razor, Doctor, trying to shave me," the patient replied.

"I was just trying to get him ready for surgery," the orderly interjected.

"John, you remember that you were shaved when you were operated on in June, don't you? It didn't hurt then, did it?" I asked.

"That was all right then, Doctor," John moaned, " but tell that barber to shave one of these other men. I done gived hair once."

"Sorry, John. You've got to do it again. You don't want an infection from your surgery because of some hair, do you?"

Assistant resident Pete Peterson joined me as we began rounds of the ward. All the other residents were with Dr. Elkhart on the floor below. We approached the bed of Elijah Brown, who was sitting upright and smiling broadly. I removed the slightly wrinkled dressing from the patient's left shoulder. The two inch long incision was clean and dry. Eight black silk stitches held the wound edges together in a slightly raised line.

"Elijah was stabbed last Saturday night, and the knife blade broke off near his brachial artery," Pete explained. "It came close to being serious."

Turning to the patient, Pete said, "Wiggle your fingers, Elijah."

The smiling patient complied. "They moves okay," he said.

"You can go home today," Pete said, "but come to the clinic next Wednesday to have those stitches taken out"

"I kinda like it here, Doctor," Elijah said. "I'd like to stay till tomorrow."

"And, how would you like your eggs cooked tomorrow morning?" Pete inquired sarcastically.

"I'd like "em scrambled, thank you, Sir."

"Elijah, this is no hotel. We need the beds for sick people, so get your clothes on and get out of here before ten o'clock."

We continued our rounds.

Assisting in surgery nearly every morning was developing my skills rapidly. I was often allowed to make the initial incision, and routinely clamped spewing blood vessels, slipped ties of catgut or silk around the stumps, held retractors to allow visibility into deep abdominal cavities, and placed and tied skin sutures. Training at The Gradies was much more thorough than the motto "See one, Do one, Teach one," but with the severe shortage of staff, both full time and visiting, learning occasionally occurred that way. I helped on several appendectomies before actually doing one myself–under close supervision, of course.

The Saturday morning CPC's (Clinical Pathological Conference) was another fascinating form of learning for the interns. A member of the house staff would read the case history of an interesting and unusual patient. After reciting the symptoms, the resident would describe the findings on physical examination, relate the laboratory and x-ray reports, being ever careful not to release information that would reveal the diagnosis and remove the mystery before the professor's analysis began. The expert then discussed the possible diagnoses and would make his final choice. One or two others might be asked to give their opinions before the hospital pathologist, Dr. Robert Mickler, who usually had the last word, projected pictures of a tumor or slides of tissue preparations that indicated the actual diagnosis.

One Saturday morning, the case of one patient with vague abdominal pains was presented. The sixty one year old white male had been in good health until three months ago. He had noticed a slight loss of appetite and a gradual weight loss of twelve pounds. Fried and spicy foods often gave him indigestion, and he had alternate bouts of diarrhea and constipation. His abdominal pains were sometimes a dull ache, and at other times, cramps. Blood pressure was normal, as was urinalysis. Chest x-ray and upper G.I. barium studies revealed nothing abnormal. A couple of blood chemistries were a little out of line, but I wasn't exactly sure what they indicated. Dr. Elkhart gave a detailed presentation of the possibilities, which included ulcer, tumor, colitis, parasitic disease, and gall bladder infection.

When Dr. Mickler showed slides of pancreatic cancer, he shocked the doctors by telling them that the slides were made from a biopsy at surgery sent from the

Mayo Clinic just last week. The patient was one of the best loved and respected visiting eye surgeons, Dr. Grady Clay. He would not be making rounds at Grady any more, and was not expected to live much longer. Disease is no respecter of persons. I remembered something my father used to say, "Every day we greet is a gift from God."

Here was another thought about God popping into my mind. Is there really a God who is trying to get my attention? I wondered.

Dr. Clay had a splendid reputation and gave of his time to teach at Grady. Age sixty-one isn't really old, either. Life and death are both mysteries. I remembered that these subjects were often discussed in Sunday school and church. It was obvious to me that individuals who were most at ease with the thoughts of death and life were those who had a strong faith, a faith that my atheism ridiculed. Every day a doctor comes in contact with both life and death at close quarters. Maybe I should give some attention to the known ways of understanding such basic questions. But when would there be time for meditating or studying such ideas? There was hardly enough time each day for eating and going to the toilet, not to mention sleeping. I would look into that later, perhaps.

OCTOBER, 1945

Dear Mom and Dad,

Things are never dull around here. I've been spending a lot of time in the emergency rooms, both white and colored, and I'm learning a lot about drunks. The police usually bring those that have passed out to the hospital rather than taking them straight to jail, in case they might actually be sick.

That reminds me of something that happened a few weeks ago. I was on the corner of Ponce de Leon and Peachtree waiting for the Shopper's Special bus—it's only five cents—to take me to Five Points. Seven or eight people were also waiting for the bus. At the back of the group, an elderly colored man suddenly fell down on the sidewalk, jerking and drooling.

The people nearest him backed away like he had rabies or the plague. I could see he was having an epileptic fit, so I turned him on his side so he wouldn't "swallow his tongue," steadied his arms, and lifted his head off the concrete until the spasms subsided. As the poor fellow calmed down and regained consciousness, I moved him over to a grassy spot to rest a bit, then caught the bus that had just pulled up. Other passengers boarding the bus gave me a wide berth as though I might spread the man's mysterious disease to them. Needless to say, I had a seat all to myself.

Back to my experience with drunks. Some are very noisy and want to thrash about. The nurses, bombarded by a lot of swear words, would like to stuff a couple of 4 by 4's in each bum's mouth, but the "bleeding heart" public would react strongly against that. Others are like cry babies. They moan and carry on and want to tell you all their troubles. A few just stagger about like a chicken with its head cut off. Even though they fall a lot, they're so relaxed that they don't hurt themselves. Sometimes we give drunks a shot of chloral hydrate to make them sleep. The ones who think they are being funny usually aren't, but others can be quite amusing. It's all very interesting, even though some of the drunks do interfere with our more serious work.

I went for a haircut yesterday. The barber said he had to go to the outpatient clinic last week because of a pain in his belly. The doctor checked him carefully, then told him not to worry. The problem, he claimed, was a fart that became caught sideways in his intestine. The barber said the doctor must have been right because he finally passed some gas and the pain was gone. He'll probably have a new story next month. Part of success in the barber business is entertaining the customers.

Next month I transfer to the medical service. I'll write to let you know how that goes. Stay well, and please continue to write.

Love,
Curtis, Jr.

A deep male voice came over the hospital intercom.

"This is administrator Wilson speaking."

Suddenly, a stunned silence descended upon the usually noisy dining hall.

Typically a female voice with a syrupy Southern drawl mixed with a nasal twang reverberated from the wall speakers. "Calling Doctor So-and-So, Doctor (first name) So-and-So," they would say. The announcement that always brought a chuckle from me was for Dr. Waldo Finger. The last name came out sounding like "fang-gah." Girls from rural Georgia are unable to roll their "r's."

Mr. Wilson continued, "All elective surgery is immediately cancelled. All interns and residents report to the White Emergency Room and ambulance entrance to receive injuries expected at once. The Winecoff Hotel on Peachtree Street is on fire and the situation is serious."

Arnold, Bill and I were seated at the same table as Amos Tutwiler.

"Where would you like us to go?" we asked Amos.

"Curtis, you come with me to the E. R. Bill, you and Arnold go with the ambulances."

Almost instantly, I could hear sirens shrieking from every direction as fire trucks, police and hospital vehicles raced to the heart of the city. As I ran out to the sidewalk, I noticed a huge plume of dark smoke billowing skyward less than a mile from the hospital.

"It must be a huge fire," I thought to myself.

The first ambulance to arrive at Grady Hospital brought two men and a woman from the hotel. Two nurses and I helped them out of the vehicle. Their soot-blackened faces were streaked with pale lines where tears from their irritated eyes had run down their cheeks. Each was coughing between gasps for breath, but fortunately their clothes showed no signs of burns. The trio had certainly been enveloped in smoke, but luckily no fire.

Amos and I, now joined by Dr. Frank Foote, examined these first victims, and quickly administered drops of the topical anesthetic, pontocaine, to halt eye irritation and the flow of tears. The middle-aged man I was attending was finally able to open his eyes and survey his new surroundings.

"Doctor, you can't believe how terrible the fire is," he said. "People were screaming and jumping out of windows in a horrible panic."

He continued to cough and wheeze, so I moved him next to a metal oxygen tank and held the plastic cone over his nose and mouth.

"Just a little oxygen to help you breathe," I said, opening the valve to deliver a flow of two liters per minute.

Amos appeared and said, "Go easy on the oxygen, Curtis, we'll probably have to use a lot before this is over. I've sent Leon to round up some more tanks."

As my patient became more comfortable and less agitated, I was able to remove the oxygen cone and inquire about his escape from the hotel fire. He explained his name was Thad Thomas, and he had awakened early, showered, shaved, and dressed to go down to the lobby from his third floor room in search of a morning paper. However, one end of the corridor that led past the elevators toward the dining room and kitchen was full of gray smoke.

"I started up the stairs to my room to get some of my things, but the stairwell was also filled with smoke. A man and woman came stumbling down the steps and nearly knocked me over. The smoke was awful."

"Stay here and breathe a bit more oxygen," I said. "I hear more ambulances coming in."

Passing nurse Ann Baker, I said, "Remove the oxygen as soon as he seems to be breathing okay."

A dark haired woman, unconscious, lay on a stretcher being pulled from the rear of the ambulance.

"What's the story on this one?" Amos asked the driver.

"Pretty bad," he replied. "She jumped from a fourth floor window. Broke her legs. I saw the whole thing. Gruesome . . ."

He continued to shake his head as he returned to the driver's door of his ambulance, climbed in, and sped off in the direction of the smoke-filled sky. I stayed with Amos and the new patient as she was wheeled into the first cubicle of the E. R.

"Pulse is pretty thready," Amos said as he placed his fingertips over the carotid artery on the side of the woman's neck.

As Amos lifted the flaccid upper eyelids to look for pupil size and reaction, I removed the blanket from the lower end of the stretcher. One stockinged foot was pointing sideways and the leg looked nearly six inches shorter than the other. The dark blue skirt appeared purple where blood had soaked it completely. Slipping the scissors from my hip pocket, I cut the dress material, peeled the edges to either side and surveyed the jagged end of the heavy femur bone protruding three or four inches from an uneven tear in the otherwise smooth, rounded left thigh. Only a small amount of blood continued to ooze from the wound edges.

Dr. Tutwiler turned his attention to the leg.

"Keep trying to get a blood pressure," he said to Nurse Baker. " I think this woman has lost a lot of blood. She's in serious shock already."

"I can't get a reading," Ann said, staring at the dial on the sphygmomanometer cuff.

"I'll start an I. V. with 5% glucose in normal saline until we can get some blood ready," Amos replied.

I inspected the woman's right leg. The thigh appeared shortened due to a slight, uneven "S"-shaped curve halfway between the knee and hip. There was movement of the lower part of the limb when I twisted the foot gently from side to side.

"This femur's broken, too."

"I can't find a vein in this arm," Amos announced.

Slipping the tips of his stethoscope into both ears and pressing the diaphragm to the woman's sternum, he added, "No heart sounds. No respiration. She's dead."

I pulled the sheet over the twisted legs and looked up at the woman's ashen, still face. The upper eyelids rested like half lowered shades over steamy windows, revealing large, dark pupils. Straight black hair, trimmed in bangs, covered part of her forehead. Ann slowly unwrapped the cuff as Amos jotted the time on the corner of the sheet for later transfer to a permanent chart record: EXPIRED 9:53 A. M.

"Do we know her name?" Amos asked.

"No, but I'll try to find out," Ann replied. "She had no identification on her."

I had seen dead people before, ranging from the formaldehyde pickled bodies that we had dissected in minute detail in anatomy class, to cosmetically decorated corpses in funeral caskets, plus several patients who had died during the night in the hospital wards, but this was the first person I had actually witnessed move from the realm of living to the dead right before my eyes. The mystery of the phenomenon was mesmerizing. Terms like "dead," "expired," "terminated," passed away," "gone," "departed," "deceased," and "slipped away" passed through my mind like the moving advertising signs at New York's Times Square.

What exactly is life? I mused. All the parts, the anatomy, are right here on this stretcher. The heart, the brain, and the internal organs are all in place, but their activity, the physiology, has stopped.

I thought back to Sunday school and church during my teen years, the Bible course at Emory University, and my senior years at the University of California, where learned teachers confidently proclaimed that total knowledge of all life's secrets was less than a decade away. Their prophecy was far from accurate since every new scientific discovery only disclosed at least two more deeper mysteries to unravel. But for some reason, I did remember words from the Book of Genesis, chapter two, verse seven:

And the Lord God formed the man of the dust of the ground, and breathed into his nostrils the breath of life; and man became a living soul.

That's as good an explanation as I've heard so far, I thought. The breath of life has gone out of this woman's body, and something real is missing.

Ann Baker took the white cotton stretcher sheet and drew it to the top edge of the cart, gently draping it over the dead woman's face.

I remembered Shakespeare's comment comparing human life to a stage on which the actor plays out a brief scene. When the play is finished, the curtain is drawn. Like the theater curtain, the thin, white sheet signaled the end of yet another short life.

Wailing sirens, banging doors, and excited voices snapped my attention back to the frantic situation at hand. I quickly checked on Mr. Thomas, who was breathing easily and anxious to leave.

"You can go now if the paper work is finished. We'll need this room for the others coming in."

As I led Mr. Thomas to the registration clerk we both had to quickly step to one side as a nurse and orderly wheeled yet another stretcher around the corner in a wide arc. Nurse Baker was straining to guide the heavily laden, wobbly-wheeled cart into the center of room two.

"What on earth is under that sheet, Ann?" I asked as I eyed the white mound that domed more than two feet high and tapered to both sides of the carriage.

"It's the biggest woman I've ever seen," Nurse Baker replied.

I flung back one end of the sheet and was staring at a pair of bare feet. The right foot did not reach the full extent of the left, and the toes pointed at an awkward angle.

"Another broken leg," I mumbled.

As I moved to the opposite end of the stretcher and turned the sheet back to better expose the woman's head, I was immediately aware of her slow, regular respirations, the closed eyelids, and the sooty smudges on her face.

Dr. Foote appeared, and I was relieved to have a more experienced resident on hand.

"The ambulance driver told me about this lady," Frank said. "If the situation weren't so serious, it would rank as an equal to a Keystone Kops comedy."

Four firemen had spotted an enormous woman struggling out of a third floor window.

"She's going to jump or fall, if she gets outta' that window," one of the men said as he yelled for additional assistance with the round canvas jump net. A fifth fireman reached the others just in time to raise the tarp to chest height and jockey themselves into position directly below the panic-stricken woman.

"Here I come," she screamed, as she literally tumbled into the smoke filled air and plummeted toward the sidewalk. All two hundred and eighty four pounds of human flesh met the net like an unexploded V-1 rocket bomb, the force of which snapped all five men into a tight pile in the center of the circle and on top of the huge human missile. The woman had landed on her side with her lower leg angled.

Just before fainting, she screamed, "Get off me. You're hurting my leg."

Fortunately the firemen had suffered no serious injuries. They unscrambled themselves, hoisted the now motionless woman into an ambulance, and dispatched the vehicle off to the hospital.

Nurse Baker reported the pulse as 76, blood pressure 138/92, and respirations 12 per minute.

"She's not in shock," Dr. Foote remarked. "Check her for injuries other than that broken leg, Curtis, and if she's in much pain when she comes to, give her three quarters grain of morphine. She'll need to go to the orthopedic service."

As Frank pushed back the curtain that served as a door, he called back, "See if you can find a vein and start an I. V. Normal saline."

Four hours later, Amos Tutwiler and I sat on one of the reception area benches. All the frantic emergencies had been cared for, and both of us physicians sipped a cool, refreshing soda. Ambulance driver Hank Butterfield sat down, removed his green cap, and wiped his forehead with a rumpled handkerchief.

"Did you fellows hear about your buddy, Doc Burnside?"

"He rode to the hotel with you, didn't he?" Amos asked.

"Is he all right?" I quickly interjected.

"Oh, he's fine," Hank said. "In fact, he's a real hero. Probably be in all the papers tomorrow."

"What did he do?" Amos asked.

"Seems he went with some of the firemen into the building next to the hotel," Hank began. "They went to the roof, hauled a ladder up by a rope, and laid it across the gap between that building and the Winecoff Hotel. All time smoke was a thick as sorghum syrup. The doc crawled across that ladder, like crossing Niagara Falls on a tightrope, and helped rescue some folks that had made it to the top of the hotel. They got out of there before the smoke got too thick and the fire too hot."

"Are you going back, Hank?" I asked.

"I'll go back in a few minutes, but when I left, the firemen said that everyone was out that was going to get out. It was really bad. It'll be some while before anyone can go in to get the dead bodies out. There's still lots of heat and smoke."

Hank shook his head. "They tell me that more than one hundred people lost their lives there this morning."

The newspapers certainly featured the fire on the front page the next day. It ranked as one of the worst fire disasters in America, not the kind of publicity any large city desires.

The remainder of the afternoon was involved with completing chart records, checking on patients who were admitted to the hospital, and restocking supplies in the emergency room.

After supper, I rested on my bunk bed and tried to imagine how doctors who had just served in World War II dealt with emergencies day after day in the heat of battle. Today I suddenly had a greater appreciation for their service and was glad I had chosen medicine for my lifetime occupation.

I think God is really trying to get my attention, I thought as I shifted my head to a softer spot on the pillow. The mystery of life and death had become a haunting theme as I thought back on the events of the day. "How did life start? And how did it become so complex? In bacteriology class I had examined tiny germs only one cell in size, yet pictures taken through extremely high powered microscopes showed many tiny organelles with varied functions inside the cell wall. And the covering membrane itself was an intricate structure that controlled what passed into or out of the cell itself. "How could something so complicated have developed by chance?"

Saturday night in the Emergency Room was always full of surprises, but that particular evening I was not prepared for the sight of a very intoxicated man being carried through the swinging doors by four stout companions, one on each leg and one on each arm. The spread-eagle patient was moaning, crying, cursing, but offering no resistance to being carried along in such a manner.

"I can't believe they did this to me," he groaned again and again. "Get it out, Doc. Get it out!"

One of the bearers tried to comfort the man. "Just be calm, Harold. The doc will take care of you. Stop complaining. You brought this on yourself, you stupid jerk."

By that time, Nurse Adams, Leon, the E. R. orderly, and Dr. Watson Waters, one of the surgical assistant residents, had gathered, curious about the commotion.

"What's the matter with your friend here?" I asked, pointing to the nearest examination table. "Just put him on the table there."

"He can't stand up, or sit down, or lie on his back, Doc. I'm not sure what to do with him."

"Why not? What's the problem?"

"It's like this, Doc. Harold, here, has a Nehi bottle up his butt. Oh, excuse me nurse. I forgot you were here."

Watson Waters stepped forward to take charge. "He's got what?"

"A Nehi bottle up his, uh, behind. The dummy got caught cheating in a poker game, and the other guys got mad at him."

"Lay him on his side on that table," Watson said. "That's the safest position."

The four men eased their burden onto the table to the accompaniment of howls, admonitions, instructions, and general complaints by the fifth member of the group. Dr. Waters slipped a rubber glove on his right hand, covered his index finger with lubricant, and pulled the already unbuckled pants down to expose the man's buttocks. A few rivulets of congealed, but undried, blood coursed an inch or two from the anal aperture onto the surrounding skin.

"Stop howling," he said. "I'm not going to hurt you."

"It hurts on its own, Doc. Please don't make it any worse."

Dr. Waters eased his finger into the lower rectum and quickly encountered a hard, smooth object. Removing his finger, he said, "We'd better get an x-ray of this."

"Don't move me again, Doc. I can't stand it."

"We don't have to move you, pal. This cart has wheels. Let's all go to the x-ray room and have a look."

After the x-ray technician had been located and awakened, the picture was finally made, and it did, indeed, reveal the presence of a tall, cylindrical object with a tapered end reaching above the level of the umbilicus.

"Better locate the anesthesiologist on call and alert the O. R. night supervisor, Curtis," Dr. Waters said. "We have to put this guy to sleep to get that bottle out."

While Miss Adams tended to the necessary paper work, including the required signature on the surgery permit, I made my way to the operating room to insure that proper instruments would be selected for the unique task ahead.

"Hi, Mary," I called out as I recognized Miss Beck carrying a bundle of sterile towels into one of the operating rooms.

"What's going on at this late hour, Curtis?"

"Give me a kiss, and I'll tell you."

"Get outta here," Mary said as she deposited the linen load, wrapped her arms around my neck, and planted a lengthy, warm kiss on my lips.

"Now, wipe off the lipstick and tell me what instruments you want. By the way, what kind of case is this?"

"There's a half drunk guy down in x-ray who needs a Nehi bottle removed from his rectum," I said, trying to maintain a stern, professional expression.

"Come on, Curtis, I know weird things happen here at The Gradies, but quit kidding and tell me what instruments you need."

"I'm speaking the truth, Mary. It's a real bottle that some friends shoved all the way up this fellow's rear end–out of sight, in fact."

"Maybe you'll need obstetrical forceps and handle it like a delivery," Mary quipped. "What will you need, sure 'nuff?"

"I don't really know, there are no clamps large enough to get around the bottle. We'll need some abdominal retractors to spread the anus. Maybe with enough lubricating jelly or mineral oil, it will slide out with pressure from above. There's probably nothing in the surgery textbooks about this. We'll just have to fly by the seat of our pants."

"Bad pun," Mary said.

"Sorry."

Forty five minutes later, the patient was on his side on the operating table, where the anesthetist had an I. V. running in his vein. Watson stood gowned and gloved, and Mary Beck opened a pack of drapes.

"Give him some pentothal, Sam, and put an endotracheal tube down. We're going to need some serious relaxation, here," Watson said.

When Harold was thoroughly asleep, Mary used gauze sponges and antiseptic soap to clean the patient's entire buttocks area. She followed that with an iodine prep. Drapes and towels were clipped into place, and Dr. Waters probed the rectum with his gloved finger.

"I'll never get a grip on this bottle if we use enough lubricant to prevent tearing the mucosa," Watson said.

"It's too thick to break and too risky, even if we could," I said.

Sam joined the conversation with a thoughtful observation. "Even if you can get a hold on the bottle to pull it out, won't it create a vacuum at the top and evert the colon?"

"You've got a point there, Sam."

Suddenly I hit upon an idea. "Why not drill a hole in the bottom of the bottle? That would prevent a vacuum. Also you could slip a hook through the hole and pull the thing out."

"That sounds like a reasonable approach," Watson replied. "Get us a drill, Miss Beck."

Mary located the sterile bone drill and placed it on the Mayo stand. Watson and I took turns grinding the reluctant glass bottom until a quarter inch hole resulted. With a narrow-tip bone ronguer, Watson enlarged the opening to twice that size. He inserted a pair of strong hooks into the bottle and firmly, but gently, slid the cylinder out of the man's thoroughly greased anal canal.

"The lacerations aren't bad," Watson said. "A few stitches should do the job. He'll have a very sore butt for a few days, but no worse than a hemorrhoid operation."

Mary Beck washed the bottle and asked, jokingly, "Do we send this specimen to the lab?"

"Heck, no," Watson said. "We'll take some photos of it and Harold, here, for proof. Otherwise nobody will believe us. Better admit him overnight, Curtis, after he's awake enough to leave the recovery room."

Having finished the necessary paper work, I slipped back into the operating room to find Mary Beck finishing the clean up.

"That kiss before surgery was so good, I've returned to beg for another one—or two."

"Any time, Doctor."

After a few minutes of very pleasant smooching in the empty room, I wiped my lips thoroughly and hurried back to the emergency room. I spent the next half hour relating the details of the unique surgery to Nurse Adams and Leon.

"My sphincter has tightened into a hard knot just thinking about it," Miss Adams said. "That man will have to be on a mineral oil diet for a week."

"I need to catch a nap, Miss Adams," I said. "Wake me up when the next taxpayer comes in for some free medical treatment."

NOVEMBER 1945

Dear Mom and Dad,

I'm sure you've read all about the Winecoff Hotel fire. Sorry I didn't write you sooner about the flurry of activity that went on in our emergency room that day. One hundred nineteen people died from smoke, fire, or injuries when they jumped out the windows. Did you see the picture of the woman in mid-air with her skirt flared out like an umbrella? Unfortunately the skirt didn't slow her descent, and she was killed. I watched her die when she was brought into our E. R. What a shame.

This month I transferred to the medical service. I'll be under the watchful eye and pointing finger of Dr. Eugene Stead. Dr. Stead has the reputation as one of the finest teachers in the country, and he is a serious taskmaster. One of the interns on the service admitted a patient sent in by an LMD (that's what we call the family physicians around town–Local Medical Doctor) about 10:00 p.m. The man didn't look very sick when he gave the intern a slip from his doctor that read "Admit for work-up. Possible peptic ulcer." The intern put the patient to bed and went to bed himself. At report the next morning, Dr. Stead looked the intern straight in the eyes, pointed his long index finger at his nose, and said, "We always do a complete examination as soon as a patient is admitted to this hospital. There are no exceptions."

The intern felt about as small as a South Georgia sugar ant.

Also Dr. Stead qualifies as a true absent-minded professor. Last week he drove to the hospital one morning, but rode the street car home that evening. When his wife asked where the car was, he remembered that he had left it at the hospital. He had to ride the street car back to work the next morning.

I didn't tell you about the student nurse I dated recently. Her name is Betty Jo Chandler, a tiny girl with gorgeous red hair, about the color of Aunt Lyra's. She's teaching me how much fun it is to neck. You probably wondered if I'd ever get around to dating and learning about girls. Now that I've found out how much fun it is, I think I'll keep on enjoying it when I get the chance.

By the way, you remember Calhoun Witham, don't you? We were in the same class at Central High. He's taking a straight medical internship, and I'll be working with him starting next Monday. I see him often in the dining room. He's just as funny as ever, seemingly without really trying to be funny.

Love,
Curtis, Jr.

Outpatient medical clinics at The Gradies consisted of a series of open-front booths with side walls that reached about three quarters of the way to the ceiling. Sounds traveled easily from one examining room to the next. Each cubicle was furnished with a chair for the patient, a six foot long examination table, where the patient could recline or sit for part of the physical examination, and a stool for the doctor. A small shelf holds exam items, and prescription pads, which patients called "scrips."

I had escorted a young adult, black woman from the large waiting area into cubicle 3. As the patient was getting settled into the single chair against the back wall, I heard Dr. Calhoun Witham's voice drifting over the flimsy partition to our left.

"Did you take those thyroid pills I gave you last month?" Calhoun asked his patient.

The female voice responded, "I took one of those pills, Doctor, and it made blue smoke float up in front of my eyes."

"That's the silliest thing I've ever heard," Calhoun said.

Before I could overhear any more of the conversation, my own patient was seated and ready to be attended.

"What sort of trouble are you having today?"
The woman swallowed hard, shifted her position in the chair and replied, "I think I has the cute disseminated lupus erythematosus."

My mouth fell open, but I quickly regained my composure and considered how to handle this surprise.

What the heck was this disease my patient had just mentioned?

Using the excuse that I needed to make an urgent bathroom call, I backed out of the booth and made a straight line to the hospital library. Finding the thick medical dictionary, I quickly thumbed through the pages to the "L's."

"Mmmm, let's see . . ."

lupulin -

lupulone -

lupulus -

lupus -

"Here it is."

Lupus-

1. Erythematosis. Usually a chronic, but occasionally acute, disease of the skin, characterized by red, scaly patches of various sizes and configuration that often induce atrophy and superficial scar formation. It is a capricious disease, the acute form of which is often fatal.

Additional description listed several mild systemic symptoms, such as low grade fever, malaise, joint pains, etc.

I returned to my patient.

"What makes you think you have acute disseminated lupus erythematosis?"

"My friend, Pansy Dawkins, was just treated for it, and I feel just like she says she did when it started."

"Tell me how you feel, Leticia," I said.

"Well, I have aching in my legs, and I think I've been running a little fever."

I went through the routines I had learned for the complete history and physical examination.

"I think you're probably just coming down with flu, Leticia. Take these pills," I said, as I wrote out a "scrip" for aspirin, " and come back Wednesday, unless you get worse with cough and high fever."

"What should I do then?"

"That'll mean you have a bad case of the flu, so take your pills and rest in bed until it goes away in three or four days."

My next patient, Maude Collier, an obese, middle aged woman with recently diagnosed diabetes, handed me her medical chart which indicated that she had been given a 1500 Calorie diet to follow.

"Did you bring your urine sample from this morning, Maude?" I asked.

"Yes, sir. Here it is."

The patient drew a small pickle jar from her handbag. The dipstick test showed 3+ glucose.

"This is worse than last time, Maude. Are you really being careful about your new diet?"

"Well, Doctor, I have to admit that it's a problem. I eat everything like it says on that sheet the other doctor gave me, but it fills me up so much that I can't hardly finish the food in my regular meals."

The rest of the morning went by without any more surprises.

At lunch, I found a seat next to the chief medical resident, Dr. Bert Duval.

"I go to the cardiac clinic this afternoon. What's it like, Dr. Duval?"

Bert Duval spooned another helping of potato salad onto his plate and said, "You'll be giving intravenous mercurials to a whole bunch of patients today. Next week, you'll get to listen to some hearts and participate in the case analyses."

Between mouthfuls, Bert added, "Some of those chronic cardiacs have only a few veins left, Curtis, so you'll get some tough practice."

Dr. Duval's prediction proved painfully true. A few patients had nice, easily punctured veins, but several displayed shriveled, bloodless veins in both arms. The diuretic drug that I was injecting had to be administered slowly and directly into the flow of blood. Even a few drops leaking from a vein and infiltrating the adjacent tissue could cause pain and scarring. Intense inflammation causes complete closure of the involved vein segment and renders it useless for future injections. I was careful to do my job as perfectly as I could.

The last patient in line was a wizened black man who had obviously maneuvered himself into that spot.

"Hello, Doctor. My name is John."

I looked at the hospital clinic record that had been offered to me by the thin, outstretched arm.

"John Washington, is it?"

"Yessir."

"Tell me, John, why did you want to be last in line?"

"Well, I'll tell you, Doctor, I've been coming here for my shots every week for about three years now. Most of my veins have been used up, and I wants to see how good each new doctor is at sticking veins before I want to risk another miss. I been watching you for an hour now, and I like the way you work."

"What would you have done if you hadn't liked my way, John?"

"No offense, Doctor, please, but I would have asked for the head doctor to stick me himself. He's really good at it."

I inspected both of John's arms and hands, noting the many scars and cord-like veins that lay beneath his thin, dark skin.

"There's a pretty good one on the back of my left hand, Doctor," John said, pointing to a small, worm-like vein.

"Let me get a smaller needle, and we'll see how it works."

"Take your time, Doctor. I'm in no hurry," John said, as his lips rolled back into a wide smile.

The old adage "haste makes waste" ran through my mind as I carefully tightened the rubber tourniquet around the patient's bony arm and palpated the distended vein on the outstretched hand.

"This little fellow rolls a bit, but I think we can hem it up by coming at it from the left side here," I thought aloud as I wiped the skin with a cotton ball moistened with 70% alcohol.

John sat at rigid attention, eyeing the needle as it eased through the thin skin and slowly moved toward the sinuous vein that was no larger than a shoe string. The flexible vessel gently moved sideways as it was pushed by the needle tip. Suddenly the sharp point popped through the vessel wall, and just as quickly I halted its penetration and directed the point along the course of the vessel as it slid back to its former location. With a gentle pull back on the syringe plunger, a drop of dark red blood eased into the clear solution in the barrel. John's body relaxed its rigid posture. I smiled and slowly pushed the therapeutic liquid into the tiny channel, after I had loosed the slip knot of the tourniquet.

"Your shot is finished. You'll be okay for another week," I said, "and this vein will be good for another shot later."

"Thank you, Doctor. I don't have many veins left in my hands and arms. You doctors may have to start on my feets if I live long enough," John replied, with a return of his wide smile.

"Curtis, have you seen that patient with orthostatic hypotension on the male ward yet?" Lewis asked, as we were finishing breakfast of scrambled eggs, grits, and toast.

"No, what about him?"

"The guy actually passes out if he stands upright and still for even a few minutes," Lewis explained. "When he walks in town and comes to a red light at a street corner, he has to walk around in circles so he won't fall down on the sidewalk. All the staff doctors are interested in his case."

"I'll check him out after morning rounds on my ward."

When I reached the female ward, a tight circle of doctors in white coats had assembled at the chart desk. Next to Dr. Stead stood Dr. Arthur Merrill, a specialist in medical diseases of the kidney. The others included chief resident, Dr. Bert Duval, assistant resident, Dr. Frank Foote, and my roommates Lewis and Arnold.

My patient, an elderly black woman with severe uremia, was in the first bed. Knowing that Dr. Merrill would be especially interested in this patient, I had memorized all the data on her chart carefully. After presenting the history, physical and laboratory findings, I described the retinal arteries.

" The retinal arteries appear narrowed, irregular in caliber, and show an increased light reflex. That's compatible with her blood pressure of 160 over 100," I said.

Dr. Merrill asked about the accuracy of estimating the blood pressure from the appearance of the retinal arteries.

"I can make a pretty good guess, but the eye resident does a much better job," I said.

"Tell me how you do it, please, Dr. Benton."

Fortunately, I had just reviewed the characteristics of hypertensive retinopathy. .

"According to the latest classification, there are four stages of severity. The first change in the arteries is an increased light reflex, making the arteries appear more shiny than normal. The blood pressure will usually be about 140 to 150 over 90 or 95. In the second stage, the arteries appear more narrow than normal, and may even be irregular in caliber. Where the arteries cross the veins, there will be an indentation, called "nicking." The blood pressure will be 150 to 160 over 100. If there are a few small hemorrhages on the retinal surface next to some small vessels, it is stage three, and the blood pressure will be 170 to 180 over 110. In stage four, the optic nerve head will be swollen, and there will be more hemorrhages and a few white patches called "exudates" or "cotton wool spots." The blood pressure will probably be 220 over 120."

"How did you learn to use the ophthalmoscope so well, Doctor?" the professor asked.

"I went to optometry school before medical school, Dr. Merrill."

"Personally, I prefer to feel the temporal arteries with my fingers," Dr. Merrill said.

He then discussed the pathologic physiology of kidney failure and the diagnostic importance of a rising level of urea nitrogen in the blood.

From patient to patient, the doctors continued around the ward. Although I had been on medical service only three weeks, I had come to really enjoy this rotation. This was real medicine, not just memorizing facts from books or laboratories or lectures. I was confident that the things I experienced on ward rounds would stay in my memory for many years.

The patient with orthostatic hypotension was on the male ward. I located Mr. Tomlinson's bed after studying the chart information. An assistant professor, Dr. James Warren, was already at the patient's bedside. Dr.

Warren was conducting research on blood pressure and planning a trip to Africa to study how a giraffe kept sufficient blood pressure in its head with such a long neck for the blood to climb. I introduced myself and asked to observe Dr. Warren's tests on Mr. Tomlinson.

Wrapping a blood pressure cuff around the man's arm, Dr. Warren measured the blood pressure in the recumbent position, and then asked the patient to stand.

"Stand behind our friend here, Curtis, so you can catch him if he should feel faint."

Dr. Warren was able to make two measurements of the pressure before the frustrated patient began to wobble and slip floorward. I caught Mr. Tomlinson and helped him back into bed.

"Interesting," muttered Jonas Warren. "His blood pressure certainly falls fast when he stands up."

John Tomlinson had been through the procedure of standing still and fainting while first one doctor, then another, conducted various measurements. One doctor counted and felt his pulse during an episode. A resident had run a continuous electrocardiogram as Mr. Tomlinson lay in his bed, sat up, and then stood erect. Dr. Henry Hardin, the resident on the eye service, dilated the patient's eyes and observed his retinal arteries as he stood, and also when he crumpled to the floor. Dr. Hardin was a strange sight kneeling on the floor shining a tiny light into the patient's right eye.

Mr. Tomlinson received no rest during the days he was subjected to numerous tests and examinations. His unusual medical condition was discussed on ward rounds, classes, and over the meal tables.

The next morning, I went by the male ward before heading to breakfast. Mr. Tomlinson's bed was empty.

A note pinned to the pillow read:

Dear Doctors,

I have gone home. I am too sick to be doctored on animore.

J. T.

In the afternoon clinic, Dr. Frank White called me aside.

"We've got a tough old farmer whose x-ray shows upper left lobe pneumonia. He needs to be admitted for treatment, but he doesn't want to stay. I have an idea, but I need your help."

"Okay."

"Fill a syringe with 7.5 cc of chloral hydrate and be ready to inject him."

I prepared the medication in a 10 cc syringe with an inch and a half, 23 gauge intramuscular needle. I returned with Frank to the booth to talk to the patient.

"Doctors, are you going to operate on me, or not? Cause if I don't need an operation, there ain't no need of me staying here."

"But, Nelson, you're sick and you need to be in the hospital so we can give you the medicine you need to get well."

"If it's just medicine, couldn't I take that at home? I don't like hospitals. People die in hospitals."

"Tell you what, Nelson, we'll give you some medicine now, then do one or two more tests before you go," Dr. White suggested.

"Okay, Doctor."

I asked the patient to drop his overalls and bend over the table. A quick jab into the left gluteus maximus muscle delivered the chloral hydrate solution deep into the tissue.

"Ouch, that stings, Doctor."

"Sorry, it won't hurt long."

Nelson re-hooked his overall straps, started to walk to a chair, then crumpled to the clinic floor. Finding a stretcher, we lifted the inert man and transferred him to a bed in the nearby ward.

Very early the next morning, I went to the male ward to do a quick review of the chart data before the daily report to Dr. Stead. I noticed the farmer sitting up in bed with a thermometer in his mouth. As the floor nurse felt the man's pulse and counted his respirations, I was reminded of a very strange event that happened a couple weeks earlier on the medical ward. A man who was admitted for gall bladder disease was told that his blood test was positive for syphilis, and he became extremely upset. The resident tried to reassure him that the disease was inactive, and that he probably developed it years earlier. The man became so upset he even threatened suicide. When the ward nurse placed a thermometer in his mouth and moved on to the next patient, he swallowed the thermometer. Upon her return, the nurse noticed the instrument was missing.

"Where is your thermometer, Henry?"

"I swallowed it."

"That's impossible. You must have it under the cover."

"I swallowed it."

The nurse searched everywhere with no success. She reported the incident to her supervisor, who questioned the patient thoroughly before reporting it to the medical resident. Finally an x-ray was ordered, and much to everyone's surprise, the thermometer was found, lodged in the first curve of the pylorus, just at the right end of the stomach.

For several days, the glass tube remained where it had lodged, unable to make it around the sharp bend in the intestine. The resident joked with the floor nurse, asking if the patient had been x-rayed that morning to determine his temperature. After a week, Henry was sent to the operating room, where Dr. Amos Tutwiler opened his belly and retrieved the unbroken and still functioning thermometer.

I returned my attention to the present.

"How are you feeling, Nelson?"

"I tell you, Doctor, I think I'll stay here a few days. I didn't realize how sick I was until I had that fainting spell yesterday."

I lay on my bed, intent on a short nap before dinner. Music was drifting from a small radio in the far corner of the room. I recognized the melody of the Waltz of the Flowers from Tchaikovsky's *Nutcracker Suite*. It was peaceful and relaxing.

Not having heard much classical music at home during my younger years, I had been suddenly surprised and attracted to "long hair" music when I first saw the Disney movie *Fantasia*. I visited the movie three more times and found that I really liked Igor Stravinsky's *Rite of Spring* and Beethoven's *Pastorale* Symphony. The visual images created by the Disney artists had become so identified with the music that I always joined sight and sound in my mind whenever I heard any of the pieces from that unique film. Just before dropping off to sleep, I visualized again the contrast between *A Night on Bald Mountain* and *Ave Maria,* the sharp distinction between evil and good. Anyone with half a brain can see that evil and good exist, but did Hell and Heaven really exist? If both are real, and a choice has to be made, it was obvious to me which I would prefer. My final image was the scene from *Fantasia* where a line of pilgrims bearing candles pushed back the early morning darkness as they walked peacefully toward a sanctuary.

DECEMBER 1945

Dear Mom and Dad,

I am truly enjoying my time on the medical service. My roommates, Bill and Lewis, say they like the thrill of doing surgery, but I'd rather do the detective work of disease diagnosis. And I'm more and more impressed with the teaching ability and wisdom displayed by Dr. Stead. The other day on ward rounds, he asked us why there were more blood vessels in our fingers than were needed for nutrition of the tissues or function of the sensitive nerve endings. Not one of us came up with the right answer. It's because of temperature regulation. We give off more heat from our hands than from any other area of equal size elsewhere in the body. Our head and feet are also locations for a great deal of heat discharge. That's why people wore night caps during winter months before the days of heated houses.

Dr. Stead is also much respected by other medical school leaders around the country. He's invited to lecture often, but he only goes as far as Duke, Johns Hopkins, New York, or Boston for short visits. Also, to our benefit, he has begun to attract other talented teachers to Atlanta. One of Dr. Stead's interests is heart failure. He has some new ideas about the actual process that causes fluid to collect in the legs, abdominal cavity and chest in patients with failing hearts. As yet, there aren't many medicines to alleviate the problem, but research is becoming very active this year.

I've had a couple more dates recently. I took out a different nurse named Mary Beck. She's good looking and has the most laid back personality. She just doesn't get upset and is such fun to be with. She's pretty popular with the other interns, also. I still date Betty Jo most of the time, however.

You'd be pleased to know that none of the interns or nurses that I've seen on nights out drink very much. We all have a highball or two to relax, but not enough to impair our ability to drive from the fraternity house back to the hospital, or to create a hangover the next morning. There are a few exceptions, just like in medical school and college days. But, doctors are somewhat of an exception to the ways of men in other types of work.

I'll have a few days off at Christmas. As you know, I receive ten dollars a month salary, but I don't even have time to spend all of that. I thank you for the airline ticket to Fort

Lauderdale to be with you for Christmas. Although you don't claim to be a superb cook, Mother, your meals beat hospital food any day. Get the turkey ready for baking. Your present to me can be the fare back to Atlanta after New Year.

My love to both of you,
Curtis, Jr.

Saturday night, December 4, 1945, would remain in my memory as long as I live. . I was resting in bed shortly after supper when the telephone in the hall began to ring.

"Hello."

"Is Curtis Benton there?"

"This is Curtis."

"This is Frank White in the colored emergency room. Can you come down and help? There are about a dozen patients who just came in hyperventilating, complaining of abdominal pains, and claiming poor vision. I don't know what's going on. Maybe something they ate. Anyway, it's one hell of a problem, and I could sure use some help."

"I'll be right over."

Getting dressed in an intern's "uniform" is a simple matter. White underwear, white socks, shoes of any color, white cotton pants with a draw string top, and white jacket with the hospital name on the left breast pocket. A quick brush of my thinning hair, and I was ready. Since I didn't wear glasses, there was no time needed to search for spectacles.

As I emerged from the underground tunnel, I could quickly see that the emergency room was jammed with people. There were patients, family members, and curiosity seekers. Police were helping the E. R. nurse sort out the true patients from the onlookers. One hysterical woman, about 40 years of age, was screaming, "I'm blind! I'm blind!" A younger woman was breathing rapidly and holding her stomach. A large black man lay unconscious on the front emergency room exam table, and another was stretched out on one of the waiting area benches.

When I located Dr. White, I asked, "What in the world is going on, Frank?"

"We're not entirely sure yet, Curtis, but some of these patients say they drank some bootleg whiskey, and it made them sick."

"What can we do for them?"

"I pumped out a couple of stomachs, but didn't get much. Alcohol wouldn't have stayed in their stomachs very long, anyway. It gets into the blood pretty quick."

I was surveying the unconscious man on the nearby table.

"His pupils are mighty big," I observed. Turning to the nurse, Sarah Barnes, I said, "Where is the ophthalmoscope? I'd like to look at the retina and blood vessels."

As I passed the beam of my pocket flashlight back and forth across the big, black pupils, I was surprised to see that there was no response.

"Here's the scope," Nurse Barnes said, as she returned from the desk area.

I bent close to the man's face.

"Miss Barnes, stand here and help shade his face for me, please."

The tiny round beam of light centered on the motionless pupil, and with a flick of the lens wheel, the back of the eye came into clear focus. Finding a bright red artery and its neighboring darker bluish red vein against the orange background, I traced the light along the vessels toward their entry point into the eye, the optic nerve head. Instead of a sharp circle of white with the large vessels funneling into a single artery and vein in the center, I was seeing an indistinct blur of white color that spilled outward onto the orange background.

"This man has papilledema or optic neuritis," I said. "Isn't that what wood alcohol causes?"

"I know it can cause blindness, Curtis, but I don't remember how," Frank said. "You're the expert on eyes. ."

"I do like to look at eyegrounds, Frank, and I have learned how to handle this ophthalmoscope pretty well," I replied. "What have the lab tests shown?"

"The lab only does a few emergency tests at night, so we've had no help from them yet. I've called Bert Duval, and he should be here soon."

More patients continued to press through the clinic door. Some were retching, some were moaning, others chanted phrases like "Oh, me, Lordie" or "Help me Jesus."

Police had arrived and were questioning the calmer family members in hopes of learning the source of the bootleg whiskey some had claimed to have drunk, but no information of value seemed to be forthcoming.

When Bert Duval entered the confusion, he cornered Frank to assess the seriousness of what was becoming a catastrophe and to plan how to handle it.

"We need to ask the lab to test for the carbon dioxide combining capacity of the blood. Methyl alcohol causes an acidosis. Even before we get the lab going, we've got to get some I. V. sodium bicarbonate into the sickest of these patients," he said.

I hurried to central supply and returned rolling a stretcher loaded with bottles of fluid for intravenous infusion.

"There's only one box of bicarbonate ampules in the entire hospital," I announced.

"I'll call Piedmont Hospital, Georgia Baptist, and Crawford Long to borrow what they have. I'll send the ambulance driver to get them quickly. Emory may be able to send us some, also," Bert said.

"I'm going to the lab," I said.

Richard Bogert was in one corner of the hospital lab studying a medical journal.

"Look at this, Curtis," he said, pointing to an open page. "This describes a simple test for blood CO_2 combining power that's pretty accurate and quick. I hear there's a lot of people in the E. R. who need to be tested."

"What a help that'll be, Dick. I need a supply of needles, syringes, and test tubes. You're going to have a lot of specimens to test in the next few hours if this little party in the E. R. keeps up."

All the house staff and nurses who were available had been pressed into service to handle the plethora of patients and establish order out of confusion. Rolling stretchers were commandeered from the white hospital, the operating rooms, and the reserve storage areas.

By morning, some fifty-two patients lay in beds or on stretchers, filling the medical wards, the available beds in the surgical wards, and even a few in the obstetrical area, plus several in the hallways.

Frank was talking to Bert Duval. "Bert," he said, "we've run out of bicarbonate ampules, and there are lots of people with acidosis. Still more are trickling into the E. R. What'll we do?"

"I've sent someone to buy as many boxes of Arm and Hammer baking soda that they can find in the market on Decatur Street. We can dump it into the D/W I. V. bottles and trust there are no serious side effects. By being careful, we can keep down the chances of infection."

"We've been able to save most of the ones who came in alive, but so far we have several dead," he added.

Henry Hardin, Chief Resident of ophthalmology, came into the ward. I approached him and said, "Dr. Hardin, I'm Curtis Benton, one of the interns on the medical service. I'm really interested in eyes. May I go along with you and learn about the effects of wood alcohol on the eyes and vision?"

"Sure, come along. You can help me take some retinal photographs with the fundus camera I just dug out of the closet in the eye clinic."

"I've noticed that many of the patients complaining of poor vision have dilated pupils," I said.

"Yes, they do; and it seems to be a bad sign," Dr. Hardin replied.

I followed Dr. Hardin around the wards. Every patient who had blurry vision or complained of blindness in one or both eyes had swollen optic nerves. Some were also very sick, but others were alert and sitting up. Pausing at one bedside, I told Henry that the elderly woman claimed to have drunk only a small amount of the deadly mixture, yet she couldn't see her hand in front of her face.

Willie Mae Jones sat on her bed with feet dangling over one side.

"Is that you, Doctor?"

"Yes, Willie Mae. Tell the eye doctor here about drinking that whiskey."

"You know, Doctor, I wasn't just taking a drink. I only had a tiny glass of that whiskey to help me take one of my medicine pills. It was just a little bit. I don't know how that could have hurt me."

Dr. Hardin checked her pupils with his flashlight and studied the appearance of the optic nerve head deep within her eyes.

"She must not be telling the truth, Curtis. She must have drunk more than a thimble full," Henry said as the twosome walked to the opposite end of the ward.

I helped Henry roll the bulky, antique model, carbon arc lamp retinal camera from ward to ward, taking photographs of the swollen optic nerve heads.

Meanwhile Bert Duval and the other members of the medical team continued to treat the sick survivors of the catastrophe with intravenous sodium bicarbonate, poured straight from the grocery store boxes into the I. V. solution. A spirited discussion ensued about the theory that ethyl alcohol will block the toxicity of methyl alcohol, thus giving the body a chance to slowly metabolize both chemicals, but it was not put to the test. Professor Stead vetoed the experiment.

I made one more round of the wood alcohol patients before slipping off to my room for the first sleep in nearly forty hours.

A total of 325 people had sought emergency treatment at The Gradies that night. Some were victims of hysteria who had not consumed any of the poisonous whiskey, but twenty six had died, and nine were left permanently blind. This was one of the largest catastrophes of its type in medical history, and certainly the most carefully ever studied. The photographs of the optic nerves came out sharp and clear. Some were requested for publication in future editions of ophthalmology textbooks. The medical department residents analyzed their test results and prepared a splendid report for several medical journals.

I later had the opportunity to examine several of the patients who were blinded by the wood alcohol. I observed that the swollen optic nerves had shrunk back to normal size, but a pallor had set in, indicating that the nerve was dying. There would be no recovery of vision. How quickly a person's entire life can be changed completely!

At lunch a few days later, Lewis looked up as I approached the table.

"Hi, Curtis, how does it feel to be a world's authority on the ocular effects of methyl alcohol poisoning?"

"That's not much of a claim to fame. How often can any doctor expect to see such cases in his daily practice?" I replied.

"Dr. Harbin was very generous to let me have first credit for the article we've sent in for publication," I added.

"Medicine is full of surprises," Lewis commented.

I awakened Christmas morning in my Florida home. Mother stood at the kitchen stove and hummed carols to the stained glass angels hanging between the flower-patterned chintz curtains in the window.

"Merry Christmas, Mom," I said, wrapping my arms around her waist and kissing her on the cheek.

"Merry Christmas, Junior. It's so good to have you home for a full week. You can sleep late every morning."

"Mom, you know that I wake up early every morning, even without a clock."

"Your dad is shaving. He should be along in a few minutes. Breakfast is about ready."

My parents kept me talking all through the meal, anxious to hear more about my day to day work and the unusual things I had encountered.

"Now that you're half way through your intern year, Junior, do you feel that it has been worth all the hard work of becoming a doctor?" Dad asked.

"You know I've never changed my mind about being a doctor since I used to dissect frogs and rats in the garage. Now that I'm almost a real doctor, the conviction is even stronger. Medicine is so satisfying. It's good for the mind, the body, and the soul. Not much is routine. You have to think all the time. There are so many facts to learn and remember, so many books to read, so many lectures to select pearls from. When it comes to examining and treating real patients, it's like detective work, maybe even harder. Our professors are so smart that they are great role models for us. They make me want to learn more and more. We're always helping people, or, at least, trying to help them. Of course, doctors live close to death. We know we can't win the battle against the grim reaper with all our patients, but we can make the final struggle easier for most who are losing the contest."

"You know, son, that we pray for you each day. It's so nice to see you looking so well," Mother said.

"Another thing," I said after breakfast as the family sat in the living room, "people are interesting. They're all different. I can't thank you enough for making it possible for me to go to medical school and to come this far along."

Evelyn wiped a few tears from her eyes, glanced at the grandfather clock in the corner and said, "Land sakes, it's after nine o'clock. Let's see if Santa left any presents under the tree."

One package for me was solid, heavy, and not much larger than my two hands held together. The red and gold paper, sprinkled with small printed snow flakes, was held in place by a sparkly gold ribbon.

"I wonder if we'll see any snow in Atlanta this winter," I said. "It snowed only once last year. We can always count on a few broken bones and a couple of auto accidents when ice forms on the streets."

Dad interjected one of his favorite observations, "When it gets so cold here that I can't get warm with one kerosine heater, I'm moving south."

"Now, Honey, you're staying right here until Jesus comes back. You can just buy two heaters if we need them."

I tore open the wrapping paper and read the cover title of the enclosed book, The Merck Manual.

"Mom and Dad, when did you learn about this book, and how did you know it would be so valuable for me?"

"I asked Dr. Crawford, the man who delivered you twenty four years ago, if he knew a book that would be helpful in your internship. He suggested this one and even ordered it for us," Mother said.

"This book has a wealth of incredible information that I can use every day. Thank you both a whole bunch."

"Junior, now that you're a full-fledged doctor, your great Aunt Mae would certainly appreciate a visit from you," Mother said.

"Fine. I haven't seen her in three years."

Mae had spent the past ten years in bed, except for trips to the bathroom or the living room for brief visits with the family. Everyone knew she was weak and frail due to "poor circulation."

"I have a weak heart, you know," was her constant complaint.

When we entered Mae's bedroom, the elderly woman was propped up on three pillows, sipping a little "pearl tea." Pearl tea, a favorite cool weather drink for children and sick folk alike, consisted of hot water, a little tea, two teaspoons of sugar, and a generous amount of warm milk. It was slightly stimulating, and not the least bit harmful.

"My stars, Curtis, you're now a real doctor," Mae said with a weak, tremulous voice. "I'm so glad you came to see me. I don't know how much longer I'll be around to see my loved ones grow up."

I observed the woman's thin arms and her parchment skin. The part of her body that was visible appeared a faint, dark blue color. I felt Mae's pulse, which was slow and steady. I palpated her carotid arteries and found them normal. Mae's eyes had the same bluish tint to the scleras that should have been porcelain white.

"Aunt Mae, do you use nose drops?"

"Not any more, but I used to use drops in my nose every day for years. I don't seem to need them any more."

"Were the drops argyrol?"

"Yes, they were so soothing."

"Aunt Mae, your heart seems to be holding its own pretty well. You just keep taking things easy, and you'll probably still be here for several more years."

I recognized that my aunt had a classic case of argyrosis, and probably never had heart trouble at all. I wisely decided to keep that knowledge to myself and not upset the status quo.

I caught up on my rest during Christmas vacation and was ready to greet the New Year when I returned to The Gradies for the second half of internship

JANUARY 1946

Dear Mom and Dad,

It was so good to be home with you at Christmas, but it's also exciting to be back here at the hospital. Something happened earlier this week that is certain to make a dramatic change in the future of medicine. You may have heard of the new medicine called "penicillin" that was discovered to be a useful germ killer near the end of the war. Well, last week we received some here. A small shot of it every four hours cures pneumonia in three days. It's a real miracle medicine. It may soon be available for private doctors if the drug companies can produce it in large quantities. Penicillin comes as a powder in a vial. The head nurse squirts 10 cc. of distilled water into the vial, dissolves the powder, and draws it into a 10 cc. syringe. Each syringe is labeled for a specific patient, and kept in the refrigerator. Every four hours the patient gets an injection of 1 cc., until the syringe is empty. Yesterday a nurse, who had never given a patient penicillin, took out a syringe that had 5 cc. remaining. She squirted 4 cc. down the drain so she could give exactly 1 cc. to the patient. Dr. Stead almost had a stroke when he heard about it. The hospital's supply of the yellow liquid is more precious than gold; ounce for ounce, far more valuable.

Did you hear that they have arrested the bootlegger who sold the poisoned whiskey here last month? His name is Theodore Hardy, popularly known as "Fats" Hardy because he's over 300 pounds in weight. He's sentenced to several years in jail, which is much too light for the great harm he caused. Though the judge found "Fats" guilty, he also said that the people who bought and drank the bootleg whiskey were partly at fault for breaking the law.

Two female patients on the ward last week got mad at each other and had to be separated. The woman in the first bed asked me to pull the curtain, then whispered. "That woman in

the next bed keeps me awake all night because she drinks R. C.
Cola constantly and belches all night like a cow with colic."
When I checked on the woman next to her, she said,
"That woman in the next bed keeps me awake all night "cause
she snores as loud as my old man when he comes home drunk."
Life is never dull here at Grady. .

Love,
Curtis, Jr.

"I haven't worn this tux since college days," I told Bill as I unpacked the black suit from my suitcase a couple of weeks after returning from Christmas vacation. "I hope it still fits."

"Mine's in the closet," Bill said. "I tried it on at home before bringing it down here last week."

Our roommate, Arnold, was getting married Saturday, January 19, and we were two of his five groomsmen. His bride, Polly, was the youngest daughter of a prominent Atlanta family, and the wedding and reception were shaping up to be elegant affairs.

"I've never been inside the Piedmont Driving Club," Bill said. "Is it nice?"

"Nice?" I responded. "It's a reflection of the high class, Old South society. They park your car, open the front door for you, and there are waiters all over the place. I went there once with Glenville Giddings, a buddy of mine in med school. It was a big family dinner."

"Why do they call it a Driving Club?" Bill asked.

"I don't know. Maybe it refers back to the horse and buggy days and driving carriages."

Bill had arranged for coverage of his assigned duty in the white emergency room for the evening of the wedding, but promised to relieve Dr. Waters before midnight. I had the entire afternoon and night off on the basis of my regular rotation schedule, so we only needed to find transportation. One of the few car owners on the entire house staff was chief resident in dental surgery, Bill

Allsup. Since he was constantly on call, and not planning to leave the hospital that evening, he graciously offered his car to Bill and me.

"It's not fancy enough for the Driving Club," Dr. Allsup said. "Maybe you could park it around the corner and walk in."

"Nothing doing," I replied. "We'll drive right up to the door like we belong there and are driving a Pierce Arrow collector car. The parking attendant will probably never see us again, anyway."

On the evening of the wedding, there were only a few cars in the parking area of the Piedmont Presbyterian Church, a brick and stone edifice on Rock Springs Road, when Bill and I drove into the lot and stationed the car next to a silver-gray Cadillac sedan.

"Not too close, Curtis," Bill quipped. "We don't want that "Caddy" owner to open his big door and scratch Bill's limousine."

We had previously rehearsed our roles as grooms-men, learned our position in the wedding party, as well as the names of the bridesmaids we would accompany. With a fresh, white carnation pinned to our jacket lapel, we were ready for the wedding guests to arrive. I was soon escorting beautifully gowned matrons to pew seats, with husbands following down carpeted aisles.

Arnold's fiancee, Polly, had dreamed of a late spring wedding with magnolia blossoms as her theme flowers, but January required hot-house flowers, mostly gladioli and carnations. As the ceremony began, the groomsmen stood on either side of the central altar steps, and each, in turn, escorted a bridesmaid as she reached the first rise after the long stroll down the central pathway. Polly had selected four beautiful attendants and a maid-of-honor no less attractive than the others. The bride, herself, was a naturally pretty girl, but in the superbly elegant white gown, she stood out as an exceptional beauty. She carried a cluster of white orchids that stimulated whispers of approval from the society ladies in attendance.

Arnold seemed a bit nervous at first, but he relaxed as he watched his bride-to-be glide forward beside her proud father. The ceremony flowed along smoothly, as my attention was drawn to the delicate, mesmerizing odor of the perfume on the girl standing just in front of me.

These Atlanta debs really know how to get themselves done up to attract boys like honeysuckle blossoms attract bees in June, I thought to myself. I remembered the college dances at which the most popular sub-debs, colloquially called "Pinks," had a continuous line of boys anxious to break in and try to whirl through the crowd for a full sixty seconds before having to relinquish their treasure to the next aspirant. The girls were masters at cuddling their head against the boy's neck and shoulder, brushing their clean, perfumed hair lightly against his chin, lips, and nose. The girl dancer's posture was a sight to behold. The left arm rested on her partner's shoulder, right arm half extended horizontally at shoulder level, and buttocks thrust backward at an acute angle.

I also thought about the favorite songs that elicited jitterbug dancing, a skill I had not mastered beyond the barest fundamentals. But it certainly was fun to watch when the real experts jumped into action.

When the minister finally said, "I now pronounce you husband and wife. What God has joined together, let no man put asunder," my thoughts shifted to the present. On cue, I escorted my partner up the church aisle to the narthex, where she split without a word, or even a nod of her head, and joined her other bridesmaid friends, all chatting like European magpies. Bill and I, not knowing anyone in the throng of guests, slipped out the side exit and walked to our car.

"Well, that's over," Bill said. "We didn't make much of an impression on those bridesmaids, Curtis.

Let's head for the reception and have some champagne and cake."

"The wedding ceremony is pretty impressive, isn't it?" Bill said, as we drove Bill's sedan toward the club.

"What especially impressed you?" I asked.

"How God gave His approval way back in the beginning," Bill replied

"Where'd you learn that, Bill?"

"It's in the first book of the Bible, Genesis. Don't you study the Bible, Curtis?"

"I went to Sunday school as a youngster, but I dumped all that when I was in college."

Just then our journey brought us to our destination.

If the parking attendant at the Piedmont Driving Club disapproved of our car, he gave no indication of it, but handed me the numbered ticket, hopped into the driver's seat and sped off to a discretely remote area of the lot.

"Look at all the furs," Bill remarked as the matrons entered the wood-paneled lobby and checked their capes, stoles, and coats of mink, silver fox, ermine, and chinchilla with the cloak room maid, who greeted many by name.

The large, rectangular reception room began to fill and hum with the noises of exchanged pleasantries. Tables at one end and both sides of the hall held trays of petit fours, tiny sandwiches, marzipan in the shapes of little fruits, cheeses, crackers, cookies, nuts, chips, and a few imported fruit bits. Two large bowls contained punch, one for those few who allowed no alcohol to pass their lips, and the other for the fastidious ladies who enjoyed the taste of spiked, fruit-flavored drinks that they sipped from clear glass cups with handles grasped firmly between thumb and index finger with the fourth and fifth fingers waving freely in the air.

Bill and I walked past the bar serving mixed drinks and soda to one of the waitresses carrying a tray of champagne in real glasses with hollow stems.

"I think this is the way I was intended to live," Bill said between long, demonstrative sips of the light golden, bubbly liquid.

"If you work hard, you may get there some day," I replied. "Lots of these patrons are successful doctors just like you're going to be."

The two interns were like sheep grazing in a fresh pasture as they eased from table to table, sampling delicacies and frequently refilling their champagne glasses. Arnold, circulating around the room to greet as many of the guests as possible, encountered us as we tried to engage two of the bridesmaids in conversation. The girls took the opportunity to slip away as Bill asked Arnold, "How'd you get time off for a honeymoon?"

"Didn't," Arnold said. "I have to be back on duty Monday morning. We're going on a trip in July. Polly's folks have a cabin on St. Simon's Island. They're letting us have it the week of July 4th."

"See you in church tomorrow morning, Arnold," Bill quipped.

"Fat chance," Arnold and I said simultaneously, as all three buddies chuckled and grinned.

As the clock ticked away the last hour of the day, many of the guests began to depart.

"We'd better be heading back to The Gradies," Bill said. " I promised Watson I'd relieve him in the E.R. before midnight."

"Okay," I replied. "I'm not making progress with any of the bridesmaids. Let's go."

The house staff parking lot was near the white E.R., and we arrived without mishap, but both of us were feeling the loss of our fine motor coordination as a result of the rising blood alcohol levels.

"Let's go through the E.R. and see if anything is going on," Bill said.

Nurse Carol Briscoe vaguely noticed the two men entering the swinging doors, but as we got closer, she stared wide-eyed and said, "Dr. Andrews and Dr. Benton, what are you doing here at this hour, and so dressed up?"

"These are the new uniforms for duty in the 'mercy room,' Carol," Bill quipped.

"In honor of the taxpayer clientele," I added.

Hearing voices, Dr. Waters came from behind the curtain and said, "Come here, you guys; I want your opinion about this patient."

I felt that my cerebral function was in neutral, but I shook my head, squeezed my eyes and focused my attention.

"The guy's unconscious. Good thing, too, or he might freak out seeing you two in those monkey suits," Watson said.

Dr. Waters recited his observations concerning the patient. "Blood pressure 190/100, pulse 60, respirations 12. No odor of alcohol or acidosis. Blood work not back from the lab yet. Pupils 3mm., round, equal, and reactive to light. There seems to be some stiffness of his neck on flexion."

I asked Carol for an ophthalmoscope.

"Mind if I look at the eyegrounds, Watson?"

"Course not. Go ahead."

I blinked my own eyes, wrinkled my face and neck muscles and really focused to push aside the chemical haze that was threatening to cloud my thinking. I slowly coaxed my hands and arms to align the tiny light beam inside the patient's right pupil and strained to focus my vision on the image I was seeing. Gradually I located the white color of the optic nerve, and became aware of two feather-shaped smears of bright red blood extending toward the periphery of the retina. The nerve itself appeared under slight forward pressure.

"I think he has a subarachnoid hemorrhage," I said. "You might want to do a spinal tap."

"How'd you get so good with the ophthalmoscope, Curtis?" Dr. Waters asked. "You handle that thing like a resident on the eye service."

"Don't forget I have a degree in Optometry, and I'm really interested in the eye signs of systemic disease."

"I'll see you guys later," I added as I turned to leave. My own vision was beginning to drift in and out of focus, my upper eyelids increasing in weight, and the floor seemed to tilt slightly. With some effort, I made my way up the steps of the intern quarters, slowly removed the tuxedo, tossed it over the chair, and flopped into bed. My last thoughts focused on Bill. If Bill Andrews felt as dizzy as I did, Carol Briscoe had better offer him some black coffee and pray for a quiet night in the E.R.

The interns and residents who were attending the Saturday morning CPC were a bit surprised, but not shocked when Dr. Elizabeth Gambrell, a senior medical student and the first female in the history of the school, approached the podium to discuss a case of meningitis. Elizabeth had taught the course in bacteriology when I was a freshman. Due to her unflagging determination to become a doctor of medicine, she had set aside her successful career as a teacher and made the plunge. Quite capable of holding her own with the younger male students, Miss Gambrell was near the top of her class and would graduate with honors in a few months.

A 23 year old man had been admitted with a headache, stiff neck, and fever. A spinal tap revealed fluid containing many WBC's and bacteria. Dr. Gambrell had supervised the culture for germs which identified the causative agent as pneumococcus. She had taken that data to the professor of medicine.

"If penicillin kills pneumococcus in pneumonia patients, it may also cure this strain of meningitis," Dr.

Stead had said when the information was presented to him. "You have my permission to try it."

In addition to intramuscular injections every four hours, a dilute solution of penicillin was introduced directly into the spinal fluid every day. The patient recovered completely in four days, which at that time was regarded as almost a miracle.

Elizabeth Gambrell thoroughly enjoyed her opportunity to engage once again in the role as teacher, and she did a splendid job of explaining the steps in diagnosis and therapy. Microscope slides were projected on the screen for all to see. I felt a tingle of excitement as I imagined what new miracles might be on the horizon for medicine.

FEBRUARY 1946

Dear Mom and Dad,

I've learned how to do spinal taps. Once a week I work in the syphilis clinic with Dr. Heyman. Many of the patients have neurosyphilis. The little spirochetes that have been in their blood for years finally reach the brain and burrow in to stay. A variety of mental changes follow, sometimes headaches, at other times a silly sort of light headedness. Some patients have what appears to be strokes, and many have some degree of blindness as the optic nerves become involved. It is quite common for the victims of neurosyphilis to have deterioration of the spinal cord with impairment of function in the legs.

We obtain enough spinal fluid to test, and that's what I've gotten pretty good at doing. The patient sits in a chair backwards so he can lean against the back of it. Fortunately, most of the patients are thin, so I can easily feel the tips of the vertebrae in the lower back. The needle is about 3 inches long, with a thin stylette in the lumen. I take aim between two of the lowest vertebrae and slowly slip the needle in the gap between the two bones. When the tip reaches the covering of the spinal cord, it meets a little resistance, then sort of "pops" through. I stop immediately, steady the needle, and pull out the stylette.

Spinal fluid - it looks like water - comes out in drops, which I catch in a test tube. When I collect enough liquid for the desired tests, I put the plunger, the stylette, back in the needle and slip it all out quickly. I missed once or twice the first day, but since then, I've been quite successful.

The other day I was coming up the front steps of the hospital when a man stopped me.

"Hey, Doc," he said, "remember me? I'm the one that got the spinal tap last week."

The man didn't look familiar to me. I had done about twenty taps last week, and Dr. Heyman had probably done even more than that. I just pretended to remember him and said, "I haven't seen the results, but they must be in. You'd better ask in the clinic."

"I just wanted to know what the test showed, Doc," he replied.

Maybe he thought he was the only patient who had his spinal fluid tested last week, or maybe he forgot how many other patients were there at the same time he was. People tend to think we doctors have an endless supply of knowledge in our heads.

Syphilis is a great imitator disease. It can affect so many different parts of the body. The first sign of infection is a hard, non-tender sore on the genitals. Men often think it comes from a break in the skin caused by the abrasion of a pubic hair, and they call it a "hair cut."

In the second stage, there is a skin rash on the body that can be confused with several other dermatologic conditions.

The third stage, which follows months to years later, can show up in a variety of organs - brain, liver, heart, nose, etc. Syphilis is called the great imitator.

It's routine to do a blood test for syphilis on all patients admitted to "The Gradies," and on any of the clinic patients where the disease is suspected. That alerts us to look for specific signs of activity. Often the infection is dormant, and a positive blood test can lead us away from a different diagnosis.

I'm sure I already told you how much I like the detective work of finding the right diagnosis.

Love,
Curtis, Jr.

On Saturday morning when the staff was meeting in the lecture hall for the Clinical Pathological Conference, the chief of the urological service, Dr. Thad Morrow, was presenting information about the ravages of gonorrhea on the female reproductive system and the results of treatment with sulfa drugs and penicillin. His opening remarks brought some surprised reactions, including laughs, gasps, and several raised eyebrows.

"Before we look at the effects of treatment on gonorrhea," he began, "we need to ask ourselves the question, 'Are we against gonorrhea, or are we for it?'"

Dr. Morrow paused to survey the audience for their reactions, then continued. "Gonorrhea is the most effective birth control measure we have for the indigent population of this city, county, and state. If we aggressively and successfully subdue this disease, we'll increase our welfare rolls by a substantial amount. Before we discuss treatment, I'd like Dr. Randy Scroggins to present a case history. Randy."

The tall, thin assistant resident on the urology service adjusted his glasses and began reading from a hospital record.

"A. W., a 19 year old colored female, presented herself to the ObGyn clinic, with complaints of intense stinging on urination. She squirmed and wiggled so much that she frequently wet the toilet seat, her clothes, and the bathroom floor. She compared the feeling to an experience she once had when she rubbed McIlhenny's Tabasco sauce on her vaginal orifice on a dare."

A subdued sound of laughter rippled through the room. Randy Scroggins had the reputation of sprinkling his chart notes with colorful metaphors and anecdotes.

Randy continued, "B. P. was 115/75, pulse 76, respirations 17. The temperature was 99.8 degrees, and the patient's forehead felt somewhat warm to the touch. When he reached the part of the history relating to the pelvis, Randy said, "The pregnant uterus was palpated and estimated to be the size of a ten cent Cuban watermelon. A moderate amount of yellow colored discharge was seen in the vulva, and the urethral orifice was swollen and as red as a Valentine heart."

Dr. Scroggins reported the results of microscopic slides and bacteriology cultures.

Dr. Morrow then took over and told how a few injections of penicillin had cleared the Nisserian infection rapidly.

Dr. Stead talked a few minutes about other infections for which penicillin had proved itself a wonder drug. He discussed how some bacteria had become resistant to sulfadiazine and speculated that others might mutate to survive exposure to the new penicillin.

"It appears to me," he said, "that we are on the threshold of an exciting new era in medicine."

As I walked back to my room, I found myself wondering if penicillin would have any effect on the more serious venereal infection, syphilis. I also began to wonder about some of the ethical considerations in medicine. Had it been right to joke about venereal disease or render judgment about who would be treated and who would not? Most people's opinions about morals and ethics were related to their understanding of the Ten Commandments. The Bible claims those laws were directly given by God to mankind, specifically to a band of wandering Hebrews fleeing from slavery in Egypt 3000 years ago. I remembered that much from my exposure to biblical history years before. Those ten rules have stood the test of time and were adopted by all of Christendom. I began to meditate on the possible result if everyone obeyed those rules completely. Society would be a hundred times better than it really is now. No theft, no murder, no venereal disease, no stab wounds or bullet holes to repair in emergency rooms. From nothing other than a practical point of view, being a Christian was obviously not a bad thing. I wondered if I had been wise in rejecting God and the Christian faith. Maybe I had only made an intellectual change while deep in my subconscious I was still inclined to embrace the beneficial teachings and heritage.

"I want to do some studies on cardiac output," Dr. James Warren said to the medical interns and residents one morning after rounds.

"I need to make some measurements on normal subjects before evaluating patients with heart failure," he added, "and I need some volunteers."

"What does it involve?" Dr. Frank White asked.

"Slipping a catheter into an antecubital vein and running the tip to the superior vena cava," Dr. Warren replied.

Bill and I, lowest two on the totem pole, found ourselves selected as the first "volunteers."

Dr. Warren had assembled his sterile supplies in the x-ray room. I lay on the cold, hard table, my chest and arms bare. As Dr. Warren scrubbed the middle of my left arm with tincture of green soap, he said," I'll inject a little Novocain and do a small cut down on this vein. It's a nice vein near the surface, so it should be easy and painless, Curtis."

The novocaine produced a slight sting, but I felt nothing of the half-inch scalpel incision. I was aware of slight pressure as Dr. Warren sponged blood that seeped from the incision lips. The vein was quickly exposed, and a black silk suture passed under it. This was tied to stop the flow of blood coming from the fingers and hand distal to the incision. Through a tiny slit in the vein wall, Dr. Warren slid in the long catheter. I could feel the tip being pushed through my upper arm, past my shoulder, and into my chest. There was no further sensation beyond that point.

I lay quietly, staring at the ceiling as Dr. Warren completed his measurements, removed the catheter, sutured the vein and skin, and applied a tight, thick dressing.

"Okay Curtis, that does it," Dr. Warren said. "We can measure how much blood the heart is able to handle with each beat with this method. That will, I hope, become a very important tool in the future study of heart function in health and disease."

After the same procedure was completed on Bill, Dr. Warren said, "Thanks, fellows. You both have a normal cardiac output. Your arms should be healed in a week. You'll have a scar as your badge of honor for being part of cardiac research," Dr. Warren concluded.

One evening, I was called to the colored female ward to work up a new admission. I chose to walk through the tunnel that connected the two buildings for white and colored patients that faced each other across Coca Cola Street, the night being rather cold outdoors.

The duty nurse handed me a nearly blank chart and said, "Your patient is in a bed out in the hall. The ward is full tonight."

I could have located his patient in complete darkness simply by following the rise and fall of a loud snoring noise. The woman, a middle-aged black, weighing a good 220 pounds, was half lying, half sitting in a bed with its head partly elevated to 45 degrees. The bulky body listed to the right, and was propped partially upright with three pillows. Saliva had formed a thin, moist line from the left side of the mouth to the chin. Thick lips hung twisted to the right of center, as the raucous breath sounds increased in intensity toward a crescendo, ceased altogether during a long pause, then resumed their noisy rise again.

"Cheyne-Stokes respirations," I said to myself. "Not a good sign."

The admission sheet revealed that the woman was named Matilda Monroe, age 47. Diagnosis—essential hypertension with CVA (cerebral vascular accident). Matilda's right arm and leg were devoid of muscle tone. I lifted the arm. It flopped down on the bed the instant I released it. The left arm offered slight resistance to being lifted, and dropped down with a tiny bouncing movement. The legs exhibited the same pattern. I placed my thumb on the right biceps tendon and struck my nail with the rubber hammer. No response. The left forearm responded to the test with a sluggish jerk.

The blood pressure cuff strained at the maximum inflation necessary to record Matilda's 240/130 readings.

"Better call this 'malignant' hypertension, certainly not 'benign,'" I mused.

I went through the routine of a complete physical examination on the unconscious patient.

Head–no scalp lesions, tremors or evidence of trauma.

Face - left side flaccid, no response to pin prick or pinching. Right side responds to pin prick and pinching.

Eyes - lids closed. Bell's phenomenon weak on left, normal on right. Eyes moderately diverged. Pupils small, react to light, both direct and consensual. Conjunctivae moderately injected. Fundus exam deferred until dilation.

Neck - no stiffness on flexion. Carotid pulses pounding. Thyroid gland not enlarged. Trachea in midline.

Chest - respirations of the Cheyne-Stokes type. Breath sounds clear anteriorly, somewhat diminished at posterior bases.

Heart - moderate left side enlargement. No murmurs. Rhythm regular. Rate 90.

Abdomen - very fat and soft. No masses felt.

Pelvic and Rectal - deferred.

Lower extremities - right leg flaccid. No patellar reflex. Left leg has some muscle tone. Patellar reflex present, but slow and weak. Dorsalis pedis pulses present in both feet.

IMPRESSION: Cerebrovascular accident, left pyramidal tract.

The patient's fat arms hid the antecubital veins from view, but I found a vein on the back of her left hand. I was grateful for the days in the cardiac clinic where hand veins were often the only ones available, and I had gained considerable confidence in tapping them. I obtained enough blood for the necessary lab tests, and then returned to the nurses desk.

"Any relatives about?" I asked.

"I haven't seen any since the patient was admitted," the nurse replied.

"No orders for now. Just keep the side rails up, and check on her from time to time."

"What's her prognosis?" the nurse asked.

"She may die before morning," I replied. "Have the night nurse call me if she does."

"Goodnight."

"Thanks. Goodnight to you."

On my way back to my room, I began thinking again about death and the possibility of some sort of life after death. The concept of a heaven in which a previously living person's spirit or soul lived on in a state of awareness seemed pretty attractive. Everyone who has mentioned heaven to me has believed that they would surely go there. Preachers were the only ones who warned people that they might go to a place called hell where constant torture awaited them if they didn't "get right with God." Rarely did a living person consider that a real possibility for himself. If I ever get the opportunity, I would like to talk to a really intelligent scholar of religion about God and the Bible.

Matilda lived long enough for ward rounds the next morning. I had instilled eye drops to dilate the pupils and examine the woman's retinal arteries before time for rounds. There was increased redness of the optic nerve heads and slight blurring of the disc margins, suggestive of some increased intracranial pressure. The retinal arteries were very irregular in caliber, gave off a glistening light reflex, and severely compressed the veins at crossings. Several small, splinter-type hemorrhages and a number of "cotton wool" patches of edema could be seen scattered about the retinas. I classified the grade of retinopathy as 4+.

Dr. Stead strode into the ward, his long white coat waving behind him. My patient had been rolled into the ward near the nurses' desk. She was the first clinical case to be presented on morning rounds. Hypertension, heart failure, and arteriosclerosis were favorite subjects of Dr. Stead. He asked questions of each of the interns and residents, and offered information about the sequence of events that led to Mrs. Monroe's unfortunate current status.

"Other than diuretics, we have only one medicine with which to treat high blood pressure," he said.

"Derived from the snake root plant of India, the rauwolfia alkaloid, marketed as Serpasil, is available in the United States. It's too late to help this patient, unfortunately. I expect research will produce several other new drugs in the next decade. We really need to have better ways to treat this very common condition. Better yet, we need to learn more about how to prevent it."

Ward rounds lasted until nearly lunch time. I welcomed the break and a quiet nap before the afternoon work began. As I walked to the dining room, I considered Dr. Stead's explanation of vascular hypertension. Clearly, obesity was a serious contributing factor.

They ought to teach that from grammar school on up, I thought. When there's no "pound of cure," the "ounce of prevention" is the most important thing we have, I concluded.

Prevention of disease received very little attention in medical school. Vitamins were regarded as minimally necessary to escape deficiency conditions like beri-beri, scurvy, pellagra, and night blindness. Encouraging patients to take multiple vitamin supplements was rare, and even, by some, considered quackery. The only weight loss programs were very low calorie diets that were temporarily successful. Smoking cigarettes was known to cause a chronic cough and emphysema, but the majority of doctors smoked regularly, and few advised patients to stop. Their own example would have inspired no one to break the habit.

Years ago a teenage friend and I acquired a few cigarettes and then rode our bicycles to a wooded area far from our neighborhood to try them out. The cigarette smoke irritated my eyes and made me feel dizzy. I was thankful that the bad experience had turned me away from cigarette smoking. I tried pipe smoking and did enjoy the sweet odor of Rum and Maple tobacco, but never learned to successfully keep a pipe burning. Even with filters in the pipe stem, the smoke had made the tip of my tongue feel raw and uncomfortable. I tossed away two pipes before the habit ever was started.

Exercise was an activity for muscle building, not as a healthy routine for men and women of all ages. My life was too concerned with corrective and palliative care to give much attention to health maintenance and preventive medicine. In fact, prevention was considered more in the realm of public health education than mainstream medicine. I was acutely aware that a short nap after lunch was a sure way to prevent fatigue during afternoon duties, and for now, that was next on my schedule.

MARCH, 1946

Dear Mom and Dad,

Today is the first day of the month, and I start on the obstetrical service this afternoon. You have heard me say that I have no desire to specialize in obstetrics. I spend the next two months on OB, then the final two on pediatrics. I think I'll like that better.

There are lots of babies around Atlanta with first names identical to several of the interns and residents here at Grady Hospital. When some of the mothers deliver their fifth or sixth child, they often hesitate over choosing a name. If the baby is a male, the intern may say, "Why not name him after me?" The mother often agrees, and the name of Bill, John, Charles, or whoever was working that shift is recorded on the chart.

We've had some cold weather lately, but I don't get out much anyway. It's too much trouble putting on a sweater just to cross the street, only to forget where I might have left it, so I usually use the underground tunnel between the white and colored units. The other day I was stopped by a teen-age fellow who was looking for the x-ray department. I told him how to find it in the white hospital, but he stopped me by saying, "I'm colored." The kid had snow white hair and very fair skin. On closer inspection, I could see his pinkish eyes and white eyebrows and lashes. He was a true albino. His hair was very curly, the lips a bit thick, and the nose slightly broad, typical negroid features. I walked him to the colored x-ray department before going on to the ward. He was the first negro albino I had seen up close.

Calhoun Witham was on the ambulance duty last month. Maybe I didn't tell you that we interns have to take turns riding the ambulance on emergency calls. It's the most dangerous aspect of our "training." Most of the drivers seem to have little regard for safety or life, neither their own nor ours. There have been several accidents, but none of the doctors have been injured—yet. Anyway, Calhoun was driven to a house where the caller had reported, "Grandmother is stuck in the bathroom in great pain." As he was led from the living room down a short hall to the bathroom door, he heard a tremulous female voice pleading with God for help. Through the already open door, Calhoun saw the frail little woman sitting on the toilet seat and wringing the skirt of her dress with both hands.

"What's the matter, Annie?" Calhoun asked. He called most older colored women "Annie," the name of the Witham maid who had been a family treasure for many years.

"Oh, Doctor, I'm having a BM that won't pass, and it hurts more than any of my four babies at their birthin'. Please help me."

The bathroom was so small that Calhoun had to lean over the hand basin to see any part of the woman's behind. Turning to the daughter, he said, "You squeeze yourself in here and take her arms and pull her forward."

With considerable maneuvering on everyone's part, Calhoun could get in a position to see a large, dry cylinder of feces protruding from the distended anus. The bowl water was lightly stained red from blood that had dripped from small tears in the mucosal orifice.

Calhoun chased the grandchildren from the door and the hall and asked the daughter to stay and help. Slipping on a pair of rubber gloves, Calhoun managed to break apart the offending impaction and dig out, piece by piece, the mass of material. A continuous chorus of "Lord, help me's" and "Oh, Sweet Jesus's" accompanied the entire procedure.

They finally got the woman lying down on a bed. Calhoun found a tube of vaseline in the ambulance first aid bag, and applied it generously to the woman's sore behind. When Calhoun tells the story to those who haven't heard it before, he makes it funnier each time and provides more elaborate details. Next time he tells it, he'll probably claim he delivered the impaction with obstetrical forceps. You know how funny he can be.

Love,
Curtis, Jr.

Less than an hour had passed since I had strolled into the colored obstetrics department when a student nurse pushed a wobbly-wheel gurney through the door.

On it writhed a black woman in her late thirties. Grunts and groans issued through her tightly clenched teeth. On seeing me, she relaxed a bit and said, "Thank God you're here doctor. This one's ready to be birthed."

It was obviously not the woman's first pregnancy. Nurse Betty Simmons had already checked the blood pressure, pulse, and temperature, and had recorded it on the hospital chart. I concentrated on hiding my nervousness as I slipped a rubber glove on my right hand, squeezed a glob of K-Y jelly on the index finger, then lifted the woman's gown with my left hand. Beneath the large, mounded belly, I located the curly, black pubic hair, and farther posteriorly, the anal opening. Gently sliding my index finger into the rectum, I encountered a firm, rounded prominence. Centered in the bulge was a soft spot about one centimeter in diameter.

"She's barely begun to dilate," I said.

Peeling off the glove and dropping it into a waste receptacle, I reached for the chart and said to the patient in my most reassuring voice, "You'll be fine. Nurse Simmons will get you ready, and we'll get this baby taken care of."

Turning to the nurse as I started out the door, I said, "You can wash and shave Mrs. Howard and move her to the delivery table."

Suddenly the patient screamed in a loud voice, "Come quickly, Doctor. The baby's coming nnnoowww!"

I jumped to the foot of the stretcher just in time to see a small head, covered with wet black hair, protrude between the woman's legs. With a few more contractions of the mother's belly, an entire baby slid out onto the white sheet of the carriage, the spirally twisted, reddish blue umbilical cord extending from the little boy's navel into the closing and retracting vaginal opening.

"I told you he was coming," the woman said.

I suddenly realized that when I examined the status of the pregnancy, the woman's cervix had been fully dilated, and what I had felt was the anterior fontanelle of the baby's head!

After tying and cutting the umbilical cord, then pressing on the woman's uterus to assist in delivery of the placenta, I noticed I was not wearing sterile gloves. In fact, no gloves at all.

"Oh, well, babies were birthed long before rubber gloves were ever invented."

"Miss Simmons, you don't have to shave her now. Just wash mother and baby and get them to a bed. I'll do the paper work."

As I wrote notes on the hospital record, I thought, Everything happened so fast I didn't think to ask if she'd name the baby after me.

My second obstetric patient was a young woman at full term with her first pregnancy. Matilda Huckabee's cervix was only 5 centimeters dilated, but the labor pains were strong and coming regularly. As I slipped on gown and gloves, I imagined this delivery would be every bit as easy as the first one. Obstetrics seemed a simple specialty thus far.

Matilda's chant had settled into a rhythm: "Oh me, Lordie, unh, unh, unh. Oh me, Lordie, unh, unh, unh."

I was busy stretching the vaginal opening and encouraging the young mother. As birth became more imminent, Matilda's heaven-directed petitions became more specific: "Oh, Jesus. Help me, Jesus." After one more severe contraction, the woman paused, then exclaimed in a loud voice, "Father, God, You better come Yourself. This is too big a job for Your Son, Jesus!"

With that, she bore down extremely hard, and her first born son propelled himself into my waiting hands. Amidst the water and mucus, bright red blood stained the white table sheet. The precipitous delivery had caused a generous tear in Matilda's left vaginal lip.

I'd get an "F" on this one if Professor Boren were here, I thought. Maybe there's more to this obstetrics than I figured.

After aspirating mucus from the baby's mouth and hearing a lusty cry, I clamped, tied, and cut the umbilical cord, inspected the baby's hands, fingers, feet and toes, face and head, then squeezed a drop of 1% silver nitrate solution into each eye to prevent the chance of gonorrheal conjunctivitis attacking the eyes and destroying the sight before the baby would have an opportunity to view the beautiful world that surrounded it. I passed the healthy baby to the nurse, then located the wrapped, sterile episiotomy kit that lay close by. Matilda was so elated over her new child that she didn't complain as I injected a generous amount of novocaine and put several large stitches into the ragged tear of her vagina.

"Now you'll be as good as new. I'll see you next year, Matilda."

"No, you won't doctor," she replied. "I ain't never going through this again."

I just smiled and recalled the chief resident's comment that most of the patients returned every year, and each told the same story about this one being their last. As I was changing into my hospital attire, I suddenly realized I had, in all the excitement, missed a second chance to have a new baby named after myself.

There'll be many more chances before the next two months are over, I mused.

One evening, as I lay on my bunk, reading an article in the New England Journal of Medicine, the phone in the "card room" rang. A spacious landing at the top of the stairs accommodated one big, round table and six chairs. Two decks of cards, one red and one blue, decorated with angels riding bicycles, provided opportunity for games of poker or gin rummy for the off-duty interns and residents. One of the card players answered the ring.

"Hey, Curtis, it's for you."

"Hello . . . Nothing special . . . I was just reading . . . What's that? Okay, I'll be right over."

The call had been from Dr. Andrew Johnson, the chief OB resident. He said there were five women in labor at the same time, that he would certainly appreciate some help, and would I mind coming over to the labor room as quickly as possible.

I slipped on my shoes, combed my hair, and crossed to the colored hospital by way of the underground tunnel. Obstetrics was on the third floor. Rather than trust the rickety old elevator, I climbed the stairs. Reaching the ward, I pushed open the door to the delivery room and realized immediately why Dr. Johnson had asked for help.

Patterned like a starburst, five hospital carriages fanned out symmetrically from the center of the room, each supporting a fully pregnant woman. Five pairs of knees angled ceilingward above five large, round bellies. A black female head on the outer edge of each stretcher emitted its individualized groans, and a cacophony of sound filled the room. In the center of the circle, on a revolving stool, sat the gowned and gloved chief obstetrical resident.

"Okay ladies, the other doctor is here, and we're ready. Who'll be first?"

I wondered if I were prepared for such an occasion. Where could such a scene be found elsewhere than at The Gradies? Quickly I changed into a scrub suit, donned a cloth cap, gown, and rubber gloves. Having first dragged another stool into the circle, I made a space for myself beside Dr. Johnson.

As the next three hours passed, first one, then another of the women delivered a baby. Much to my relief, no two precipitated at the same time, so I could be of assistance, but never completely responsible for the total care of any of the five deliveries.

One of the three little boys was given the name of John Curtis Stewart at my urging.

When all the mothers and their babies were safely in their beds and cribs, I redressed in whites and headed back to my room. Not only did I have no desire to specialize in obstetrics, but I thought I'd never be able to adjust to the irregularity of the hours required. Babies were born with the frequency of rain showers in August at The Gradies.

After lunch, a call summoned me to the ambulance door of the E. R.

"What's up, Hank?" I asked the driver.

"Seems some woman's about to have a baby at home. She has four other kids and no one to look after them if she comes to the hospital. Also she has no transportation of her own and no friends with a car. We'll have to take care of her at home," Hank replied.

"Let me check the OB supplies, and I'll be ready to go,"

The house was only a few miles from the hospital, and I was relieved that Hank refrained from trying to set a new speed record with the old green ambulance. When we reached the small, frame house that had long needed a fresh coat of paint, two mongrel dogs yapped at the strangers entering their yard. A wire fence kept the animals from reaching us, though they hopped against it and barked ferociously. A young girl opened the door.

"Mommy's in there," she said, pointing to a room near the rear of the house.

The young mother, not yet starting her fourth decade of life, lay on a disheveled bed and stoically managed her labor pains.

"It'll be here soon," she said. "I'm glad you made it in time."

Hank had "assisted" at several home deliveries during his seventeen years as an ambulance driver. He immediately set about getting pans of hot and cold water, located towels, and engaged the children in conversation while I opened the OB kit and slipped on gown and gloves.

In less than an hour, I had successfully helped a seven and a half pound baby boy into the world. As I completed the delivery of the placenta, all four children gathered around the bed. The bloody lump of placental tissue lay in a bowl at the foot of the bed, and the children took a serious interest in it.

"What'll we do with that?" one little girl asked.

The older brother said, "We can throw it in the garbage. It won't go down the toilet."

The oldest sister thought for a minute, then came up with her own unique solution. "How come we don't just feed it to de dogs?"

APRIL, 1946

Dear Mom and Dad,

I'm still stuck on the obstetrical service. For certain it's not the specialty I wish to pursue in my medical career. However, I am getting better with the deliveries, for which the patients should be grateful. If they only knew that I'm a novice. But women have given birth to babies with little or no help for thousands of years, and even today they don't need much more from us doctors than a few kind words during the process.

In the out-patient department the other day, a rotund, middle-aged woman appeared, complaining of pain and discharge from her vagina. Dr. Johnson checked her chart and noticed she had been in for an examination three weeks earlier. He put her on the exam table and aimed the bright beam from the lamp on her perineum. A silver reflection caught his attention. On closer inspection, he saw a complete, metal, bi-valve speculum resting in her vagina. It was covered with heavy secretions, and smelled awful. With careful manipulation, he eased the appliance from its resting place and inquired how it happened to be there. At the end of her last visit, the patient thought she was finished when the nurse left the room for something. The woman proceeded to step down from the table and left. She was so fat that she hadn't seen the instrument or felt its presence. Obviously, she hadn't attempted sex since her last visit.

You know how interested I am in the eyes. I like to examine the blood vessels in the retina (inside the eye) of the women with high blood pressure late in their pregnancy. The small branch vessels often become quite narrow and irregular in caliber. Some even leak blood plasma into the retina, causing bright white patches like cotton wool. The medical condition is called "eclampsia," and can be very serious. Sometimes Dr. Johnson calls me to look at a patient and help him decide if an inducement of early labor is needed. That makes me feel rather important.

The dogwood trees are really putting on a show this month, and are dressing the northeast part of town, especially near Emory University, like a polka dot garment. The newspapers are showing lots of pictures of the blooms. They seem to get more spectacular each year.

Love to you both,
Curtis, Jr.

Obstetrics was turning out to be more than just delivering babies. There were diseases specific to the female reproductive system that I learned to recognize and treat. Minor surgery in the clinic included dilatations of urethral strictures, removal of genital warts and polyps, and cervical biopsies. Major surgery in the operating rooms ranged from Caesarean sections to removal of uterine fibroids - called "fireballs" by the patients - to complete hysterectomies. I assisted on several operations and was allowed to do a few of the less complicated procedures myself.

One aspect of obstetrics that did bring pleasure to me was watching the joy that most mothers, especially the new ones, experienced when they held their babies for the first time. Mother love is a powerful emotion and wonderful to observe.

MAY, 1946

Dear Mom and Dad,

This month and next month I'm on the pediatric service. My roommate, Arnold Burnside, has applied for a residency in child care. He hopes to work at the children's hospital here in Atlanta. Says he has always liked kids, and seems to have a way with them. After only a few days on this service, I can understand Arnold's attitude. Some of the little tots are cute. They sure can get sick quick, but they often respond rapidly to treatment. Others, who have chronic conditions like a kid named Danny Oates with osteomyelitis (a bone infection) in his left leg, begin to regard the nurses as part of their family. Danny has learned to beg, smile, roll his eyes, make promises and other tricks to get favors, such as extra desserts, rubber gloves blown up as balloons, rides in wheel chairs, etc. But there are others, like Willie Turner, who resists everything, especially shots. It requires an army commando squad to draw a little blood for tests. Willie probably hasn't had a happy home life, and his parents seldom come to visit him.

There is a separate unit for patients with polio, and most of those are children. It's a small building across the street from the nurses' quarter. We all wear caps, gowns, and masks when we go in there, and we all wonder how much risk there is of catching the dreaded disease ourselves. We practically wash the skin off our hands coming and going and in between each examination. So far, no doctors or nurses have caught it here. It is so sad to see the patients with paralyzed arms or legs, and especially those with whole body involvement. We feel helpless, knowing there's not much we can do to help them. There's a new treatment with hot packs advocated by a Sister Kenny in Australia. The idea is to keep the muscles toned up so that, if the nerves recover from their paralysis, the muscles will not be shrunken or scarred and unable to respond. The treatment includes manipulation of the joints to prevent contractures and deformities. You know how FDR liked to spend time in the hot water at Warm Springs.

By the way, "Fats" Hardy, the bootlegger who sold the whiskey containing the wood alcohol last Fall, "escaped" from jail. It seems he had been elevated to the status of a "trusty" and given the job of holding a red lantern to warn motorists on a road between Georgia and South Carolina that a bridge was washed out by a rainstorm. He got tired of standing there in the cold, damp night air, so he put the lantern down in the road and walked away. He turned up two days later in a hospital in South Carolina with a broken leg. Can you imagine jeopardizing the lives of motorists by counting on a crook to perform such an important task?

Love,
Curtis, Jr.

After supper, I returned to the pediatrics ward to check on a child who had been admitted in the late afternoon. Five-year-old Tommy Aycock's rasping respiration could be heard over the entire ward and into the hall. I approached Dr. Charles Morse, the chief resident in pediatrics, anxious to learn more about the treatment of the common childhood infection called "croup."

"It's not the amount of noise we worry about," Charles said, "it's the chest retraction on inspiration, the oxygenation level of the tissues, and the general state of toxicity."

We watched little Tommy as he coughed and rasped. His chart graph indicated a slowly rising temperature, now 101 degrees.

"I think it's time we put him in an oxygen tent," Dr. Morse added.

The square plastic affair attached to two metal rods that extended over the crib from the left side was roomy enough to reach from Tommy's head down as far as his waist and from one side of the crib to the other. The transparent plastic allowed adequate visibility for doctors and nurses to evaluate the child's condition from several feet away. A heavy, green tank of oxygen, brought to the bedside on a rolling dolly, stood at the head of the crib and was connected to the tent by a rubber hose. Charles opened the valve to allow the fresh, cool gas to flow into the tent at a rate of one gallon per minute. Tommy's breathing quickly became noticeably less labored. The nearly constant barking cough slowed, then quieted.

"What exactly is croup?" I asked.

"It's an infection of the larynx and bronchi that comes fairly quickly and starts with a very noisy, almost continuous cough. The air passages produce a heavy mucus that doesn't come up with the coughing, and that compromises the air exchange. There is also fever and toxemia, but the most important problem is swelling of the vocal cords and the lining of the larynx that can be severe enough to result in asphyxia and death."

"Do you ever have to do a tracheotomy on these kids?" I asked.

"Yes. Have you seen one done?"

"I've seen an elective tracheotomy, and I've done an emergency one by myself."

"By the way," Charles said, "if you see an older child having difficulty breathing, but not coughing much, and with no history of a foreign body, think of epiglottitis."

"Epiglottitis? I've never heard of that."

"When you see the signs and symptoms I just described, look beyond the tongue and down the throat, using a laryngeal mirror, if you have one. If the epiglottis is swollen, pale, and real big, watch out! The kid could die quickly unless you do a trach," Charles added.

"Thanks, Dr. Morse. I'll try to keep that in mind."

"Just call me Charles."

We moved closer to Tommy's bed and found him sleeping, though coughing some, and still showing a bit of retraction of the notches above and below the sternum on inspiration, but generally much improved.

"Go on to bed, Curtis. He'll be okay now. I'll see you tomorrow."

Dr. Morse and I were finishing afternoon rounds the next day when we reached the cribside of a young boy who was slowly turning from side to side and twisting the positions of his arms and legs. His flushed face, closed eyes, open mouth, with saliva trickling from each corner gave evidence of a severe throat infection.

"He was admitted about lunch time," Charles said. "Tonsillitis. Worst case I've ever seen."

Dr. Morse steadied the child's head while I directed the beam of my pocket penlight beyond the wooden tongue depressor. "Those tonsils almost meet in the midline, and are they red!" The child's temperature registered 105 degrees.

"He's had a shot of penicillin that I begged from the medical department, but it may be too late to help," Charles added. "He's extremely toxic and tiring fast."

I rested the diaphragm of my stethoscope on the boy's chest and heard breath sounds in front, then in back. "He doesn't seem to have any pneumonia."

"No, there's been no cough. Just fever and toxemia. There's nothing else we can do."

Both us doctors stood and watched as the little boy weakened steadily, until he finally made no further effort to breathe. The child became still, and the reddish flush of face and neck faded into a pale gray.

"I hate to see kids die," Charles said.

"Do you ever get used to it?" I asked.

"The older pediatricians on the visiting staff say they learn to adjust to it, but it always causes a sad hurt that hangs in the memory for a long time. Personally, I feel worse for the patients and their families when there's been some severe, permanent disability remaining that they have to live with every day."

"Let's contact the boy's family and break the bad news to them."

The newborn nursery was located on the obstetrical floor. Dr. Morse had asked me to meet him there to make rounds.

"We've had a few "preemies" lately that have developed eye problems, some even becoming blind. The eye resident says the trouble starts in the retina. He thinks that baby over there has such a problem. Would you like to look at it?" Dr. Morse asked.

"Yes, I would, but I'd have to dilate the pupils first. Let me put some drops in now, then by the time we finish rounds, it should be ready," I responded.

We reviewed the chart of each baby, discussed the findings, and made observations. We both wore surgical gown, face mask, and cap. Extra precautions against infection were always observed in the nursery. Several of the rectangular bassinets received oxygen from hoses attached to the ubiquitous green, metal tanks. Most of the tiny infants slept peacefully.

"Many of the prematures come from mothers who have had no prenatal care," Charles commented. "We save most of them, but some are just too tiny to survive. The ones with some congenital defect usually don't make it."

Dr. Morse kept up a running commentary that resembled a medical lecture, and I concentrated on learning and retaining the new information that bombarded me like machine gun fire.

"This one is being tube fed because its sucking reflex hasn't matured enough to take nourishment from bottle or breast. The nurses have to turn that one often because the lower portion of either the right or the left lung keeps collapsing when it lies on that side. We have to keep these bassinets warm because the smallest ones don't have good internal temperature regulation yet. See how yellow this one is? The mother gave birth at home and didn't clamp the umbilical cord right away. The excess red blood cells from the placenta caused the production of too much bilirubin. It should clear in a few days."

After a complete tour of the rows of babies, I located the ophthalmoscope and attempted to look into the eyes of the tiny tot that had been marked "suspicious" by the eye resident.

"The pupils are well dilated, but it's sure hard to hold these tiny eyelids open," I said.

The little circular beam of light passed through the clear cornea and clear lens and focused on the retina. I located the optic nerve, which looked normal, then followed the arteries and veins outward toward the equator of the eye.

"There seems to be lots of small, tortuous blood vessels out in the periphery," I commented. "Dr. Harbin says that those bleed into the vitreous and cause retinal detachment. He saw one baby with the retina in a tight ball right behind the lens. The eye was hopelessly blind."

"What do you think causes it?" Charles asked.

"Dr. Harbin didn't know, but it happens almost exclusively in babies weighing less than three and a half pounds at birth who survive with the help of oxygen and I. V. fluids. Do you want to look?"

"I've tried before, but I can't see much through one of those darned scopes," Charles replied.

"Seems like a good research problem," I observed, as we removed our masks, caps, and gowns, and started for the dining room for an early supper.

As we dined, Charles told me how one of the pediatricians on the visiting staff handled an overanxious mother with a child who was not very sick, but who needed mostly bed rest.

"To prevent the mother from telephoning three or four times during the day with senseless questions, he would give her a large bottle of a very dilute sedative. He would then carefully instruct the mother to give the child one half teaspoonful of the liquid every twenty seven minutes and call him when the bottle was empty."

"Every twenty seven minutes?" I asked, then laughed as the significance became apparent.

"Exactly," Charles smiled. "It would have the mother occupied all day just keeping track of the time, plus the bottle would last 24 hours."

"Another thing is his treatment for infant colic," Charles said, after reaching for a second helping of collard greens.

"Tell me about that one."

"Well," continued Charles, "the anxious mother would call about bedtime. Dr. Sims would tell her to get a bar of Ivory soap—it had to be the 99.44% pure brand—and carve a strip one fourth inch square and one and one quarter inches long, insert it as a suppository into the child's rectum, then call when the child expelled the soap sliver."

"Gosh, how long would that take?" I asked.

"That's just the point," Charles continued. "Often the family didn't have Ivory soap on hand, so the father would have to find a late night drug store and buy some. Next, to carve a strip of soft soap into the required shape without breaking it was a near impossibility. Once the suppository was in, it caused so little reaction that it was seldom passed before the next morning. Dr. Sims would have gotten a good night's sleep."

"I guess that's part of what we call 'the art of medicine,'" I said.

JUNE 1946

Dear Mother and Dad,

This note will be very short. What a splendid and exciting year this has been. The time has gone by so quickly, and it's hard to realize how much has transpired. I'll be finished with my intern year this month and will start my residency in Eye, Ear, Nose and Throat next month. The Army is letting me stay here for that. I'm excited about that.

Love to you both,
Curtis, Jr.

"Hey, Charles," I called to Dr. Morse as he entered the pediatric ward, " that little kid Willie Hankerson has me puzzled."

"Why?"

"Well, he came in last night with fever and sore throat, but he complained more about pains in his legs than soreness in his throat. He points to his joints like a patient with arthritis."

"Did he complain of any stomach pains?" Charles asked.

"Yes, he did. Once or twice."

"Is he anemic?" Charles added.

"His RBC was 3.2 million, and his Hgb was 9."

" The kid has sickle cell anemia," Dr. Morse stated with an air of finality. "Let's get a blood smear and search for sickle cells."

"We have a blood smear slide that we used for the WBC and differential," I said. "Do you want to see it?"

"That might not show much," Charles said. "To verify the diagnosis, you have to put a drop of fresh blood under a cover slip and seal the edges with Vaseline so oxygen can't get in. Then the red cells will sickle if Willie has the disease."

With considerable effort, due to the strenuous protesting by Willie, we two doctors did manage to puncture one finger tip and obtain two drops of blood on a glass slide. Charles gently placed a paper-thin cover slip atop the blood. The red liquid quickly flowed to the four corners and sides of the glass. Charles spread a thin strip of vaseline on all four sides, and strode off to the lab to locate a microscope.

Under the bright light and magnification, he and I could observe numerous red blood cells elongating and assuming the shape of a banana, or the sickle that decorates the flag of the Soviet Union. The diagnosis was confirmed.

"So Willie has sickle cell anemia," I said. "What can we do for him?"

"We'll just try to make him comfortable until the present crisis subsides," Charles explained. "If the anemia becomes severe enough, a blood transfusion will be necessary, but there's no real curative treatment for the disease."

After a lunch of roasted chicken, turnip greens, and mashed potatoes, I made my way to the library to read about sickle cell anemia. Little Willie had received the sickle gene from both parents. He had the full blown condition, which includes the anemia, the sudden stomach pains, and the discomfort of arms and legs. In addition to disintegration of one or both hips, he could develop worse problems with infection, or strokes, or kidney failure. The textbook section concerning treatment indicated that blood transfusions from time to time help the anemia, but do not cure the sickling trait. A child with only one gene for the sickle cell disease will not exhibit anemia, but may have slight bleeding from a kidney occasionally.

Hearing my name paged, I returned the book to the shelf and walked to the phone.

"This is Dr. Benton."

"They want you in the colored emergency room, Hon," the operator drawled.

Dr. Watson Waters greeted me as I entered the swinging door.

"There's a child here I'd like you to see. She has a cough and a peculiar wheeze."

The little girl was making a dry, hacking sound behind the drawn curtain. The anxious mother stood beside the even more anxious girl, as the child lay on the examining table, her body flexing with each cough. The inspired breath made a high pitched wheezing noise. At first, I failed to notice that the wheeze did not accompany every respiration, but it soon caught my attention that every now and again the breathing was smooth and easy, only to be interrupted with periods of squeaky sounds and more coughing. The child did not feel the least bit feverish.

"When did this start?" I asked the mother.

"Only about an hour ago," she replied. "She was playing on the floor near the kitchen table while I was washing some dishes. She started coughing and gagging, and she threw up once. When I heard that funny noise in her chest, I brought her here."

As I started to place the stethoscope on the little girl's chest, she grabbed her mother and clung tight.

"That's okay," I reassured the woman. "Just pick her up and hold her. I can listen to her back first."

I could hear air expanding the lungs, but it made a high pitched noise as it did. The sound was what is interpreted as "dry," with no moist bubbling element. As the girl cried, there was no hoarseness or signs of laryngeal edema. I listened to the chest a bit longer, then stepped out from the cubicle and approached Dr. Waters.

"I think the girl has aspirated a foreign body. Why don't we get a chest x-ray and call Dr. McMath, the ENT resident?"

"Would you mind doing that? I have to stick to the patient in the next room pretty closely," Watson said.

Half an hour later, Dr. McMath and I were scrubbing our hands outside the operating room. The pungent odor of tincture of green soap hung in the air over the large porcelain sink.

"Have you seen a bronchoscopy yet, Curtis?" Will asked.

"No."

"Well, I'll explain everything to you as we go along, in case you have to do the next one."

A gauze covered wire mesh cone was being held over the child's nose and mouth as she lay on the stark white operating table. The intense smell of ether permeated the room and the anesthetist held a small tin can of the volatile liquid a few inches above the mask and gently let a trickle of drops fall on the gauze.

"She's pretty well under," the nurse anesthetist said, as she prepared her machine that could pump ether vapors through a rubber hose into a "J" shaped metal tip that could be hooked into the girl's mouth, or from the hose directly into a tiny projection of the bronchoscope that would feed the fumes deep into the lungs.

We slipped on gowns and gloves, draped sterile towels over the child's neck and chest, and clipped another towel around her head. Selecting an appropriate size child's scope, Will hyperextended the girl's head and slid the illuminated tip of the long, slim cylinder over and alongside the tongue, while lifting upward.

He let me peer through the tube to visualize the vocal cords as they alternately widened and narrowed in the shape of an inverted "V." Glimpses of the trachea, with its cartilage rings, was exciting to me.

"I'll slip the tip between the cords as they open wide. Never try to force the scope through, or you might injure the epithelium and cause later swelling. That could be worse than the original problem."

Deftly, Will slipped the bronchoscope beyond the larynx and into the trachea for a distance of two or three inches.

"You were right, Curtis," he said. "There is a foreign body. Take a look."

I placed my eye near the outer end of the instrument and saw a flat, dark object wedged in the very beginning of the right main bronchus.

"It looks like some sort of seed," Will said. "It's too wide to fit into the scope, so I'll have to grasp it and remove it trailing."

Extending his right hand toward the nurse, Will said, "Foreign body forceps, please."

Nurse Beck slapped the long, thin, metallic instrument with a scissor type handle into the doctor's palm. From the tiny tip extended two fine wires, angled at their very tips into minute points that opened and closed like crab claws. Will slid the forceps through the scope's hollow center. Just enough space remained for visualization of the unwelcomed object in the airway and the forceps' teeth. Skillfully and gently, he opened the claw tips, slid one over and one under the seed, and squeezed them closed. As he slowly pulled back the forceps, the seed came along until it reached the far end of the bronchoscope, where it stopped abruptly.

"Mustn't pull too hard and loose your grip, or break the seed into smaller pieces," Will said. "That could compound your problem."

"I think it's a watermelon seed," he added.

Rotating the forceps ninety degrees, Will turned the seed vertically, and, keeping it snug against the end of the scope, slowly and steadily pulled both upward, out of the trachea toward the vocal cords.

"Let's hope it stays hooked," Will said, as he eased the scope and the seed between the vocal cords and out of the child's mouth.

"That was exciting."

Will examined the watermelon seed and showed it to the scrub nurse, Annie Beck, to the circulating nurse, and to the anesthetist.

"Well, Curtis," Will said, "now that you've seen one bronchoscopy, you're ready to do the next one."

Later, after I had changed from the scrub suit into white pants and jacket and was walking back to the pediatric ward, I thought about some of the highlights of my internship year. I was glad in one way that the great war had stripped the hospital of most of its staff. That had meant very hard work, with long, exhausting hours, but what a wealth and variety of things I had seen and learned. I had also completed many types of examinations, treatments, and even surgeries that in normal times would have taken two or three years to accomplish.

One thing about The Gradies, I thought, it may not always be "teach one," but it certainly is often "see one - do one."

I was ready to start the next phase of my training.

CHAPTER 3
GIVING BACK TO MY PATIENTS

Starting practice 1948

The first chance at repaying the debt to the many patients who had allowed me to learn my skills on them came at the start of my private practice. I could and should start at once.

On graduation from medical school, my class recited the Oath of Hippocrates, which contained these words, in part: In purity and holiness I will guard my life and my art.

Whatever house I visit [or whoever attends my office or hospital or clinic] I will come for the benefit of the sick . . . be they free or slaves [or today, descendants of slaves].

On my office wall also hung a plaque containing the mission statement of Dr. Thomas Sydenham (1642 - 1689), which ends with the words: The doctor being himself a mortal man, should be diligent and tender in relieving his suffering patients, inasmuch as he himself must one day be a like sufferer.

I vowed to always give my patients my best efforts on their behalf.

Race segregation was still evident in 1948 when I opened my office in Fort Lauderdale, Florida. There were drinking fountains labeled "white" and "colored," but society had moved quite a long way on the road to full integration, and I was determined to treat both black and white patients equally since both had contributed equally to my learning. Wanting to show both how much I appreciated them. I made no distinctions in appointments, charges or treatment.

Routine office visits were only five dollars in those days. A pediatrician once referred me a patient who paid my fee in cash after the mother had paid him with a large basket of beans. Dr. Dobbins kidded me about that frequently throughout the years that followed.

An important aspect of showing appreciation to current patients for what their predecessors had given to me is making a constant effort to keep on schedule with appointments. As hard as any doctor tries, it's not always possible to avoid getting backed up in the later hours of the morning or afternoon. We cannot predict how complicated some patients' problems are, but one factor we have some control over is to start on time. A sure way to get behind is to begin behind schedule for the first appointment. Recently some patients have filed lawsuits against doctors who have kept them waiting a long time without explanation or apology. My father used to put a fictitious name in his appointment book in mid morning and one each afternoon. That allowed him to have a cushion for unexpected delays. I never used that system, but I respected my patients' value of their time and knew they didn't appreciate undue waiting to be seen.

For many years I developed a subspecialty of pediatric ophthalmology, so I made some special accommodations for them in my waiting room. In addition to a few small chairs, I placed a leather-covered, soft-stuffed rhinoceros, large enough and safe enough to be sat upon and played with. Another item that children enjoyed was a large wood carving of a head, two feet tall, anchored in a marble block too heavy to move. The wood was smooth and finely polished with no chance of splinters harming little fingers. The head, that of a Negro boy with mouth open wide, was named by the office staff African Choir Boy.

Throughout my entire career I tried to think of each patient as a representative of those on whom I worked in my training years and what I owed to them. I did my share of charity work, taking turns on call for hospital emergencies, participating in a free cancer clinic that the local medical society sponsored, and even making house calls to shut-ins and patients in nursing homes who were unable to come to the office or hospital.

In 1958, a friend physician and I built a shared office on a busy boulevard that ran from the center of town directly to the beach. On a few occasions, a loud metallic crash heralded an auto accident on the intersection just out our front parking lot. I always hurried out to the scene of the wreck in case any medical help was needed. Once a young man on a motorcycle was struck by a car. As I came upon the scene it was obvious that medical help was needed—and fast. The unconscious youth was fast choking on blood in his mouth and throat. By rotating his head, reaching in his mouth to pull his tongue forward, I cleared his breathing passages and kept him alive until the ambulance arrived. A few days later I received, unexpectedly, a Citizen of the Week award and a write up in the local newspaper for what most any doctor would have done in similar circumstances.

In those years we physicians had no thought about AIDS or HIV infections and didn't mind getting blood on our hands. I also looked down many a broncho-scope into a lung filled with tuberculosis. God certainly spared me from many dreadful diseases.

A concept I didn't possess in the early years of my practice became valuable to me in the later years was inspired by Dr. Francis Schaeffer, a friend whom I came to know and love. Fran had said he visualized every individual he encountered as a person made in the image of God and therefore of infinite value. It was not always easy to keep that concept in mind, especially with difficult, cantankerous patients, but I tried.

When I began practice in Fort Lauderdale, I was assigned a number, 56, the 56th physician to start practice there. That designation had to be used when public announcements were made, calling for a given doctor to answer a phone call at a ball game, for example. This was long before the era of cellular phones. This eliminated the ruse of staged phone calls to publicize names.

I was active in the work of the Broward County Medical Association and was elected president in 1965, the year Medicare was under consideration by Congress. That was a busy time for the some 300 doctors then practicing in the area. By the time I left Florida, the number of physicians was over 1200. In those early days, we all knew every member, and we would invite the entire membership to parties. I felt an obligation to all members of my profession as well as to the patients for their success of the profession in general and our local society in particular.

In the area of my speciality, ophthalmology, I felt it important to work on a state wide level to help uphold the public image. I was elected president of the Florida Society of Ophthalmology in 1974, and contributed my share of time and effort in those endeavors.

I was able to help repay God through my profession by helping found the Christian Ophthalmology Society in 1977 along with Dr. J. Lawton Smith and Dr. Ron Seeley. Our goal was to encourage young students and new specialists to keep their attention focused on the place of God in their practices. From a small start of about 30 members, the Christian Ophthalmology Society has grown to a nationwide organization with annual meetings, a regular publication and over 600 members. It helps support ten missionary eye projects in foreign countries.

CHAPTER 4
THE U. S. ARMY EXTRACTS ITS POUND OF FLESH

My practice grew, and everything was going nicely for nearly three years, until the U. S. Army decided it was time to collect on the debt I owed it.

I remembered back to the day our class was inducted as a group into the Army at Fort McPherson in Atlanta in 1943. We were lined up on the parade ground with an equal number of assorted recruits from the pool of other young men. A long time, salty old sergeant was addressing the new soldiers. Pointing to several large trash cans scattered about the open area, he barked, "These is G. I. cans, and they is not made to be sit on."

He continued, "Now all you ERC's take two paces forward."

We students were called the Enlisted Reserve Corps. Our class stepped forward from the line up.

"Now you ERC's pick up all the cigarette butts and other trash and put them in these cans. The rest of you recruits watch closely and learn how to do this. These ERC's are all college graduates and they are smart."

On another occasion when we were all inside our sleeping building, the sergeant explained the meaning of a bell to us.

"When you hear this bell, you are to go outside and line up in front, and don't mess around getting out there. When this bell rings, I'll give you thirty seconds, and I want these barracks solidly empty."

On the final day of our induction, our favorite sergeant was making a speech to us and another group of fresh inductees.

"Now I want you to know I'm not a horse's ass. . . ." As he continued speaking, Archie MacAllister, standing next to me whispered, "I'm sure glad he told us that. I'd have gone away from here thinking he was."

Back at school things returned mostly to normal, except every week or two someone from the military would assemble our class in Coca Cola Place, a street that ran along side the hospital, and have us march back and forth to keep us mindful of our connection to the service. The war was over soon after we graduated, and everyone had scattered their separate ways.

I was extremely fortunate to be offered the position of Research Director of the newly established Clay Memorial Eye Clinic in Atlanta, established at Grady Hospital in memory of Dr. Grady Clay. This would substitute for service at some Army hospital. Not only would I be back in familiar territory, but I would be able to expand the knowledge of my specialty.

Although I didn't realize it at the time, this move must have been planned by God as He knew He would draw me to His side years later.

After putting my equipment in storage, informing my patients, referring those in need of continuing medical care, telling friends "goodbye," Margaret and I departed for Atlanta with our one year old daughter, Janet, to serve out my time. Knowing my stay in Atlanta would not be permanent, we rented an apartment and quickly readjusted our lives in the familiar environment.

The next spring, Margaret gave birth to a boy. It was a lengthy and difficult birth because the baby was in the breech (head in the upper womb instead of down in the birth canal), but the baby was able to be turned around in the final hours before delivery, which proceeded without further problems. We named him Dudley, my middle name. Margaret had wished for a red headed child, and one look at the baby let her know her wish had been granted. Years later as he was teaching classes while obtaining an engineering PhD degree, he grew a foot long red beard that he had to shave off when his baby daughter discovered it was a fun thing to pull on with both hands.

One way to learn a subject thoroughly is to teach it to others, and part of my new responsibility involved teaching the senior medical students about the eye and its diseases, especially as related to general medical diseases. There are so many general medical conditions that have symptoms and signs that show up in the eyes, and one of them, diabetes, has today become a leading cause of blindness in America. One of my classmates Arnall Patz, who also had obtained a degree in optometry before entering medical school, became chairman of the department at Johns Hopkins and developed the laser treatment of diabetic retinopathy that has saved many people from blindness; Dr. Patz received the Presidential Medal of Freedom in 2004 from President George W. Bush for his outstanding contributions in the field of ophthalmology.

My time at the Research Clinic was very important in furthering my education, and when the Army issued my discharge in 1952, I was ready to return to Fort Lauderdale and resume my practice.

CHAPTER 5
PAYING BACK MY FATHER
With a trip around the world and an African Safari

AUGUST 8 - OCTOBER 10, 1959

The opportunity came for me to repay, in part, my father for some of his contribution to my medical education. A close friend and colleague, Dr. Malcolm Miller, a transplant from Ohio who had been accustomed to deer hunting each fall in his former location, had booked a safari in East Africa for September, an adventure he had dreamed about for years. Malcolm had invited a dentist, Dr. Clayton Konas, to accompany him, and suggested I come along. Learning that four could go as easily as three, I suggested asking my father to fill out our team. When Dad agreed, I got busy planning a trip around the world for both of us to have a major adventure. Dad and I would travel westward through Asia and meet Malcolm and Clayton in Nairobi in September to start the safari.

My father at age 61 was not considered by me to be an old man. I remember an occasion at a summer camp in North Carolina when I was twelve. On the last day of camp, we kids were demonstrating our new skills to the parents who had come to pick us up and take us home. We were to climb a free hanging rope some twenty feet up to a tree limb. I made it up using hands and feet like a monkey.

"May I try that?" asked my dad.

"Sure, Dad."

He climbed the rope hand over hand in half the time I had taken. I was being duly impressed.

From Fort Lauderdale we flew to Chicago and boarded one of the first jet airliners in America to cross the continent to Los Angeles. We arrived on the west coast in about half the usual time required for such a trip on the conventional propeller driven crafts.

As our Pan Am Clipper took off toward Hawaii, I settled back and thought about my dad. Weighing 140 pounds,–as he said, "soaking wet"–I couldn't figure out what difference a little water would make. He was all bone, skin, and muscle–not a pound of fat on his lean body. My father was a serious person, always the reliable one in his family with an older brother whom he helped in employment and a sister born with one hand missing. He had put himself through optometry school after marriage and having two children. He had learned to relax a bit and enjoy fishing, orchid growing and golf after moving to Florida at age 45 to recover from chronic brucellosis (undulent fever contracted from unpastuerized milk). I was glad his health had improved, and here we were together on a great adventure.

With an early morning landing in Honolulu, we had to eat breakfast before our room at the Moana Hotel was ready. We were greeted at the hotel by Mr. Ephraim Field, an architect working for the Navy and a member of the Christian Business Men's Committee. I had written to him before the trip, asking if we could meet in Honolulu.

"Welcome to Hawaii," he said. "God has brought you safely here."

Mr. Field drove us around to show us some of the island's beauty, especially the view from the top of Punch Bowl mountain. We remarked how similar the foliage was to that of South Florida. Famous Diamond Head Mountain gave us a nice panorama of the island.

There are more women tourists in Hawaii than men. We figured many were widows. All the tourists, both men and women, buy the most outlandish multi-colored outfits, wear straw hats and hang flowers around their necks. Most appear very obvious among the city's pedestrian traffic.

Surfing in Honolulu is popular, and Dad was willing to try it with me. We weren't very skilled at the sport and spent more time paddling out to the waves than coasting in, never managing to stand erect, but resting on hands and knees. We only succeeded in getting our backs sunburned.

Hawaii is well known for lauaus as great tourist attractions. We signed up for one, along with about 500 other guests.

"Look who's here," I exclaimed as I spotted Ernie and Reva Hall, friends from Fort Lauderdale. We chose seats near them and commented on the smallness of the world. The fresh fruit was a delight. Seeing a piece of meat on my plate, Dad asked, "What's that?"

"Roast suckling pig," I replied. "We've had it with some Cuban friends at home. It's good. Try some."

Taking a few bites, Dad agreed, "It's better than bacon."

One speciality from Hawaii was poi, a sauce that looked like wall paper paste and tasted like I imagined wall paper paste would taste. A coconut sweet for dessert was really nice. A hula dance show was a nice conclusion to the evening.

In a Buddhist shrine the following morning, we refreshed our memories about that faith and were able to ask questions of a girl lecturer. Heaven and Hell exist only on this earth and in this life in Buddhist theology. The only thing considered permanent is change. Dad and I regard Buddhism more as philosophy than religion and it seems to fit well with the calm, oriental spirit.

At the next evening meeting of the Christian Business Men's Committee, I was the guest speaker and my subject was the paradoxes of God–such sayings as to be great, one must be a servant, and to find life, one has to lose life.

Crossing the Pacific in a Pan Am Clipper Ship, we passed the International Date Line on a Tuesday night. Awakening on Thursday morning, Dad seemed somewhat disturbed.

"I've completely lost a Wednesday, my favorite golf day," he said.

Landing on Wake Island, we had an hour to walk the beach and view some of the remains of World War II, which included the hulk of a Japanese ship protruding from the water near the beach and an airplane propeller sticking up in the sand.

We left the flight in Manila because we planned to visit a dear friend missionary named Spotty Spotswood. Spotty served in the southern Philippine island of Mindinao, and had established many new churches there. Owning and operating a one engine airplane, he was able to visit remote areas and had developed a much respected reputation. His visits to Fort Lauderdale had made a significant impression on me, and I was anxious to get a closer look at his mission field. Spotty met us in his Jeep at the coastal city of Cotobato as our flight from Manila landed there. We learned why Spotty needed a tough vehicle as we bounced over the rough "highway" to his station in the center of the island at the "city" of Kidapawan.

Dad and I learned about rice growing as we traveled along. New rice is planted thickly in flat fields that are afterward flooded. When the sprouts are about one foot high, they are thinned by transplanting most of the straight green plants in other fields. These sprouts then grow four or five feet tall, turn golden in color and develop the seeds near the tops. Usually harvested by hand sickles, the cuttings are stomped by barefoot farmers, then tossed into the air on a breezy day to separate the husks from the good rice. After being polished, it is ready for market.

When first preparing the airstrip behind his house, Spotty encountered a huge boulder in the middle of his planned runway. The rock was ten feet long and six feet wide, too big and heavy to be moved by pushed by hand or even with the help of his jeep. Spotty set out to beat the rock into smaller pieces with a heavy sledge. His neighbor, a simple farmer came over and said, "What are you doing?" Spotty explained his problem, and the neighbor said, "I'll get rid of that rock for you."

The Philippine farmer had no formal education, but he did have a wealth of practical knowledge. He, with Spotty's help, dug a huge hole in the earth adjacent to the rock, let it roll over into the pit, and smoothed the soil over the top. The airstrip was perfectly level when I took off on it with a flight with our host a few days later.

Just north of the mission rose Mt. Apo, highest point on Mindinao. Spotty wanted to visit a mission church beyond one shoulder of Mt. Apo the next day. Another American youth pastor who was visiting at the same time joined Spotty and me and four other church workers on the hike. One Filipino was the pastor who hiked there each week to hold services. Arriving mid afternoon, we were greeted and served bottles of orange soda that were very refreshing. There were no shops or stores anywhere in the village, and we knew that everything had to be brought in by backpacks. That made the soft drinks especially appreciated.

After Spotty preached a message in the village church, I was asked to see a patient, an elderly woman with a painful eye. My flashlight revealed a corneal ulcer. Having no medicines, I suggested cleansing with sterilized, boiled water and warm compresses. Our prayers also helped and the woman was better the next day. Thirty or forty young people had gathered for teaching, games, and play.

Fatigue helped me sleep on a thin straw mat on a plain wood floor that night. We returned to the mission the next day.

While I was hiking with Spotty, Dad had the opportunity to visit with Mrs. Spottswood, Mariam, and the five Spottswood boys, Curran, David, Steven, and a pair of twins, Paul and Philip, ranging in ages from 6 to 18. All the boys were helpful in showing Dad around the mission and the neighborhood. The men neighbors were Muslims and short, scarcely five feet tall. My father stands 5' 11" and towered over his new acquaintances. The village chief is called a "datu." He had four wives and a brother living in his home. They all lined up with Dad to have a picture made. Dad was also able to get a little rest and write some letters home.

Spotty flew Dad and me to Davao City on the east coast to catch a flight back to Manila. I was sitting in the co-pilot seat, and Spotty said, "Curtis, you fly the plane for a while. I want to read this newspaper." He showed me how to steer the craft, how to use the foot controls and the steering wheel, then sat back relaxing. "Keep looking out for other air traffic and don't hit anything," he added.

It wasn't hard keeping the plane on a straight, steady course, but that was my first, and only, turn at flying an aircraft. I was happy for Spotty to handle the landing in Davao.

"The Hong Kong airport closes at one hour after midnight and the employees go home. We're putting the plane into high gear and expect to make it on time. Hold onto your seats."

As our Cathy-Pacific prop-jet left Manila in the late afternoon, the pilot said something like that over the intercom. We did land before the witching hour, and learning that the famous Peninsula Hotel could not give us a room, Dad and I got a comfortable room at the Astor Hotel where we had a partial night's sleep.

The tourist hotels are actually on the mainland section of the city named Kowloon. The Star ferry shuttles across the mile wide bay to Hong Kong Island where nearly a million people live, many being refugees from Red China to the north. A cable car took us to the top of the mountain where we got a panoramic view of the city.

The fascinating Tiger Balm Gardens was built by a very wealthy Chinese man who made big bucks selling a very popular analgesic ointment containing menthol and camphor called Tiger Balm. The park is crowded with cement animals, dragons, gods, and human figures in vivid and gaudy colors. Across the hillside is a mass of pitiful shacks where thousands of refugees eke out a meager existence. Men and women, dressed in black coolie garb, wearing sandals and conical straw hats trudged along the streets carrying heavy loads on their shoulders or backs. They were road builders or repairers. The men are paid ninety cents a day; the women seventy five. Daily food costs about sixty cents. We Americans too often don't think about how fortunate we are to live in such luxury as we do.

On the south side of the island is beautiful Repulse Bay with a lovely beach. Thousands of boats with whole families living aboard jam the harbor. The Sea Palace, a large double-decker floating restaurant was reached by water taxi. We ate a delicious lunch, then returned to our hotel in Kowloon to board our afternoon flight to Bangkok.

The Bangkok airport is fifteen miles from the city, reached slowly on a pitted, congested road. Our room in the elegant Oriental Hotel was much appreciated.

We watched the morning traffic on the river as the day began while eating breakfast in the restaurant facing the water. Motor boats dragged barges with families in residence. Women poled small crafts loaded with vegetables or goods for sale.

Much of Bangkok is devoted to Buddhist temples and priests. Young men may choose to be monks for life, but many elect to serve for one week, one month, or one year. With shaved head, dressed in the easily recognizable saffron colored robe, each carries a small black bowl to receive offerings of food. Eating an early breakfast, they eat again at noon, then fast until the following morning.

Married men, serving as priests, leave their wives completely for the period of their service. The priestly duties include prayers and care of the temples.

One temple features a tall statue, the Standing Buddha, another a reclining Buddha, but most have seated Buddhas with legs crossed and one hand in the teaching posture. One rather small temple housed a solid gold statue of Buddha about six feet tall. It was said to have been made about 700 years ago and covered with cement to prevent theft by marauding enemies. It was recently discovered when a farmer was moving it from his land and some of the cement chipped off. The figure was dazzlingly shiny. Most statues were gilded, but with the gild wearing off in ten years, there was plenty of work for priests to repair constantly. Many of the temple roofs were decorated with small fragments of colored glass or china that reflected the sunlight in all colors of the spectrum.

At the Pasteur Institute spectators stood behind a three foot high concrete wall and observed snake handlers walk among hundreds of lazing cobras, picking up one here and there to milk their deadly venom into a glass jar. The snakes are fed once a week with buffalo milk thrust down their throats from long glass tubes. The huge, ten foot long, king cobras were fed one inch squares of buffalo meat from tongs in a similar manner. My own grandmother was treated years ago with cobra venom for intercostal neuralgia. Dad and I were content to stand behind the wall to watch the handlers pick up the raised up cobras, hoods flaring, with practiced ease, but pretended carelessness.

The legislative palace was modern style Italian marble and exceptionally beautiful Thailand art. Nearby was the palace where Anna, the British maiden, tutored the King about whom the recent movie was filmed.

The day ended with our attendance at a program of classical dance and music. The dancing girls were extremely graceful and beautiful.

Most of the Thai people were clean, quiet, and mild mannered.

Being so close to a seldom visited archeological wonder, Angkor Wat, we decided to make a side trip to see this remarkable place. A short flight from Bangkok went daily to Siem Reap. The DC-3 had bench seats and no floor carpet. When the plane sped down the runway, all the hand luggage that had been stored under the passenger seats slid to the rear of the aircraft in a jumbled heap.

Dad and I were two of the only six tourists who were taken to the Grand Hotel, the name more elegant than the actual building. As we rode the small bus to the ruins, we learned something of the history of Angkor Wat. The city and funeral temple, constructed about 700 years ago, deserted and grown over by huge ficus and banyan trees, was rediscovered about one hundred years ago. It was a mammoth job to clear away enough vegetation to expose the ruins, which are mostly intact and still a marvel to behold. The two hundred foot high temple in the center is decorated with faces of the Buddha and numerous Hindu gods. Dad and I climbed to the top and passed carvings of men, soldiers, animals, women with large, bare breasts, and flowers. The extent of the carvings is tremendous. Returning to the hotel, we found all our room keys laid out on the stairs. Thieves must be unknown in Siem Reap.

The next day, after a free elephant ride at the hotel, we all again boarded the bus to see the main city ruins named Angkor Thom. The Bayon, a structure with fifty tall columns containing four faces of Buddha smiling in four directions, wards off sickness and harm. The city of Angkor Thom, is surrounded by a moat. The pyramids of Egypt, Greek and Roman temples, and the Inca ruins, defy the imagination when we realize that no modern machines were available to assist the thousands of slaves or devotees who labored in the building.

Across from the city is a large athletic field with a long terrace with bas-relief elephants carved along the wall. The royal family had these choice seats for sporting events. A very large swimming pool provided room for the king and his three hundred concubines to soak and swim.

One section of the ruins, called Ta Proben was left mostly as it was found to illustrate how great was the task of clearing the hundred foot tall trees and roots running into every crevice.

Back in Bangkok, we had a morning to visit the Temple of the Emerald Buddha. The two foot tall figure is actually carved of green jade. It wears a beautiful gold crown.

The afternoon flight arrived in Singapore in early evening. We had been gaining hours on the sun with each move westward. Reservations at the famous Raffles Hotel provided a spacious room with separate sitting room and bath. Having planned only one day here, we crowded everything possible into it. An excursion by private car to Johore, across a mile long causeway, took us to the Sultan's palace and gardens. We passed a beautiful golf course, the zoo, and an orchid farm. Dad was especially happy to see the seven foot high, prolific vanda orchids to compare to his much smaller plants he grew in his hot house at home. At a rubber plantation we stopped to examine the trees and feel the rubbery latex that dripped from sliced tree bark into collection cups.

The roads were an example of British construction that contrasted with the miserable ones in Thailand. The Western spirit is much different from the Eastern, which emphasized other values, more personal then public. The Aba Baku mosque, built in Victorian style, was in contrast to typical Muslim style, but did contain minarets from which recorded prayer calls sounded two or three times a day.

At the Botanical Gardens a troop of semi-tame monkeys entertain the visitors by taking bananas from their hands and scampering about playfully. There is also a Tiger Balm Garden in Singapore, similar to the one in Hong Kong with strange and colorful statues of humans, animals and demons. We also toured the home of the rich Chinese owner, who had died four or five years ago. His sons now own and live there. The house contains a collection of jade carving, over one thousand of them, valued at more than a million dollars.

A nearby Buddhist temple featured a series of murals depicting the life of Sidhartha Guatama who became the Buddha when he obtained full enlightenment.

As we were checking our airline tickets, we discovered Dad's passport had not been stamped as we entered the country. A quick trip to the immigration office happily corrected the problem.

The airport in Singapore is one of the world's most beautiful. We arrived early the next morning, and boarded the seven hour flight that brought us to Ceylon, now called Sri Lanka. We were met there by Mr. Fernando, a member of the Christian Business Men's Committee International. He took us to the Galle Face Hotel, then chauffeured us on a afternoon trip around the city. Mr. Fernando is a third generation Christian. His wife was a Buddhist, but converted to Christianity before they married. He is the assistant collector of Internal Revenue for the island and the father of five children, four boys and one girl.

Seeming to tear through the crowded streets, we scattered pedestrians by the hundreds like pigeons. Near the city boat docks we were joined by two Hindus, who offered to put on an act with two cobras. We paid forty cents to watch them. One man put a cobra around his neck while his partner opened a large basket and played his flute as a second cobra raised his head, neck flaring, and struck half heartedly at his knee. The first man offered his cobra to me. Confident he had plucked its fangs, I took the serpent and let it crawl over my arms and shoulders. Dad is so scared of snakes in general that he forgot to snap a picture!

Whenever we approached a cow on a city street, we had to carefully drive around it for the cows, and indeed all animals, are sacred to the Hindus. Coming to Mr. Fernando's home, we met his wife before moving on to the zoo, where we saw a good elephant show. One elephant not only picked a handler up with its trunk, but also with its mouth.

Dinner at the Fernando's home gave us the opportunity to talk about how Christianity is spread in the East. The CBMC in Ceylon offers a correspondence course that has eight hundred new applications each month. We talked of foreign aid and learned that American machines were putting some laborers out of work and receiving financial aid caused some to quit trying to improve themselves and develop their own leadership. We also found it interesting to talk to a young Buddhist priest who had been converted to Christianity through the correspondence course.

Early the next morning Mr. Fernando picked us up for a drive to the city of Kandy, seventy five miles inland. We learned two more important things. First was about tea growing and harvest. Ripe tea leaves are picked every eight to ten days year round. Tea bushes are only waist high and do not require ladders to reach high nor strained backs from bending low.

Second, we learned how cashew nuts must be extracted from their thick coverings, then roasted to make them edible.

On the trip we passed several elephants working on the road or in nearby fields. We stopped once to have our picture taken with the elegant beasts.

Reaching one mountain called Adam's Peak, where tradition relates that Adam left his footprints on the top, is now under Buddhist control, and worshipped as Buddha's footprint. The "print," seventy two inches long, is decorated with semiprecious stones and mother-of-pearl, and yearly many pilgrims make the difficult climb up to the shrine.

On the shore of Kandy Lake sits a run down temple called the Temple of the Tooth, containing a portion of Buddha's molar nearly three inches long.

The University of Ceylon is to be moved to another site rather far from Colombo. In this year 1959, there were only 1600 students at the university level in all of Ceylon.

On the road we passed a communist rally, complete with flags and banners and a loud speaker blaring to the crowd. This was exactly thirty years before the collapse of that political system that held power over a significant part of the world then.

At lunch in Kandy, we ordered curry that was said to be "mild" for visitors and ones with a sensitive palate. The Hindus have asbestos-lined mouths and eat extremely hot food as common fare. The "mild" curry burned my mouth such that I was happy not to be using a paper napkin.

Dad and I thanked Mr. Fernando for his extreme hospitality on our return to our hotel.

The following day we departed on a flight that landed to refuel in Madras and Bombay, India, Karachi, Pakistan, and Aden before reaching our main destination, Nairobi, Kenya.

The manager of White Hunters, Africa, Ltd., Colonel Robert Caulfeild was accompanied by the two who were to guide our safari, Glen Cottar, whose father and uncle were famous hunters before him, and Ronnie Babault, a young pilot with the anti-poaching police. Dr. Malcolm Miller and I had hunted with both Glen and Ronnie two years earlier, and we were very happy to have our two friends again. This safari was to partially repay the enduring debt to my father so let me tell you a bit about our adventure.

Malcolm and Clayton met us at the popular New Stanley Hotel. They had checked our rifles that had been shipped earlier and reported that everything was in readiness for the trip. Parties of four clients were forbidden in Kenya, so we drove south into Tanganyika (now known as Tanzania), just south of Mount Kilimanjaro, well known by the writings of Ernest Hemingway and Robert Ruark. I had recently read the book Uhuru and was interested to know that Jomo Kenyata, who was later to become the prime minister, was presently residing in jail in Kenya.

When the tents were pitched for our first camp, Dad and I shared one and Malcolm and Clayt were to sleep in the other close by. That first night, Dad and I learned that we had to get to sleep before our buddies in the other tent did or move our tent to a more remote location. Malcolm produced a loud, rhythmic snoring while Clayt snored in a pattern known medically as Cheyne-Stokes respiration. His snoring would start rather quietly, build up to a great crescendo, then stop completely. Just when we feared he was dead, Clayt would start again in the same pattern. That first night, Dad and I stayed awake until exhaustion overtook us.

The very first day of hunting, Clayton shot a magnificent elephant with tusks weighing one hundred pounds each. He had the ivories shipped home and displayed them in his dental office.

"How would you like a tooth ache with one of those," he often quipped to his patients. Game birds, such as guinea and francolin, were plentiful, and we all shot several to supply food for our crew of twenty one national, two guides and four clients, lots of stomachs to fill each day. Malcolm informed the cook he was allergic to fowl and was served steaks from a Grant's gazelle he had shot that second day.

At our first camp, Dad bagged a big tom leopard, a nice lesser kudu, and a near record tiny antelope called a dik-dik. It's horns measured three and one half inches. He kept the head mount to display at home later. Malcolm also shot a leopard from the same bait and blind Dad had used.

At our first camp we became acquainted with the fabulous baobab trees which grow to an enormous size. Some hollow trunks have openings large enough for native poachers to make camp inside. The giant trees appear to have been planted upside down by God, the limbs looking like roots spread out near the top above the bare trunks. In season the big pods contain brown, kidney shaped seeds with a light pithy dry coating that has a somewhat lemony taste when sucked. The baobabs live a very long time, possibly five hundred years. We also learned to recognize and avoid the wait-a-bit thorn bushes. Its branches are armed with thorns that curve backward like little fish hooks and they halt one's forward progress if caught walking by. One has to reverse direction to get disentangled.

Our second camp was in the Great Rift Valley. We hunted buffalo in some head-high, thick grass. Frequently we heard the beasts crashing around, but none were visible. Once Glen and I came upon a lone buffalo bull in an open enough place for me to get off a shot. Hit in the lung, but not ready to give up, he dashed to a clump of heavy bush to rest. Glen and I waited also, then approached. The buffalo dashed from one hiding place to another while taking quickly placed shots from us both. Finally he charged.

"Take him, Doc," Glen said rather casually. I'm out of bullets."

Glen had used both barrels of his .500 Weatherby, but I still had one bullet left in my .458 Winchester. My last shot brought the buffalo down about five yards away. A year or so later, my picture with the dead buffalo was printed in the local newspaper. A young girl patient saw it and told her mother, "Here's a picture of Dr. Benton."

"Are you sure, honey?"

"Yes, it's Dr. Benton, and he's killed a cow."

The next day Dad shot a buffalo in some very thick stuff as it charged him head on. We were both surprised at the sudden encounter, but we were thankful that Dad was ready. Malcolm also got a buffalo on a small hillside that same day.

Clayton had an amusing encounter with a lesser kudu. The animal was running across Clayt's path at a good clip. Swinging his rifle to give the animal a slight lead, he fired only to see the bark of a small tree fly in splinters. The second bullet found its mark, and Clayt collected a nice trophy. There were steaks for everyone in camp that night.

In that second camp we encountered the tsetse fly, which has a nasty bite. They are a nuisance only in the daytime, fortunately not active when evening came. We were told that only one in 50,000 carry the dreaded sleeping sickness. Insect repellent kept most of the insects away during the day.

At the supper table one evening, Malcolm said to Ronnie, "You know how the Hollywood movies portray Africa as a place with a snake behind every bush. I've tramped miles and miles in this bush country and I haven't seen one snake. Where are they all?"

Ronnie replied, "But Doc, we weren't hunting for snakes."

At the next camp, I shot a record book sable antelope with forty inch curved horns. Malcolm shot a greater kudu and a big eland. The eland steaks were the best antelope meat we tasted the entire trip. Clayton added a roan antelope and a hartebeest to his trophies. Dad and I each shot a warthog. When running on fast moving legs and short steps, the wart hogs carry their tails straight up, and they are a real challenge to hit when going full tilt. Their large tusks make handsome letter openers or handles for corkscrews.

A few days later we passed through the city of Tabora and took hotel rooms for the night. At the splendid dinner, Dad asked for coffee with the meal. He was informed that coffee would be served after dinner in the lounge. The waiter was adamant about that. Some folks back home think of Africa as only jungle and wild animals!

Cool mornings led to warm, sunny afternoons, delightful weather for us. We made our last camp near Lake Victoria on the opposite end from which the Nile River originates. There was lots of plains game in that area, and we all rounded out our list of trophies, a total of twenty one for the four of us.

It was a splendid safari, and I was glad my father was able to complete it successfully and enjoyably.

We all flew to Rome to begin our journey home. Malcolm received a cable informing him that his daughter was getting married in four days. He elected to return without delay. Dad and I took a bus tour of the city, while Clayton went off the visit a friend. I especially enjoyed the marble carvings by Bernini in the Borghese Gallery. The Roman forum and the Coliseum were impressive. St. Paul's Outside the Walls was peaceful and the magnificent St. Peter's Cathedral makes a lasting impression on one. The next day we had time for a visit to the Vatican Museum. There is enough there to spend weeks and still not see it all. We ended the morning with a viewing of the magnificent Sistine Chapel.

That afternoon we flew to Lisbon, Portugal, with a landing in Madrid, Spain.

Lisbon is built on several hills that slope to a river which forms a natural harbor near the ocean. The fish market was in full swing. Women buy large baskets of fish and peddle them in neighborhoods. The fruit and vegetable market was rather large and clean and contained many attractive items. After a big lunch and a short nap, we took a taxi to Villa Franca de Xira to watch a bull fight. In Portugal, the bulls are not killed. The matadors operate on horseback to place their picks in the bull's hide, then the toreadors go through their routine of running the bull into the red cape. Finally a group of young boys enter the ring and entice the bull to charge. One boy jumps onto the bull's head between the leather covered horns. Other boys pile on until the bull is weighed down to the ground.

The final day we toured the summer palace, the Queen's Chapel, the resort seaside city of Estoril. A visit to a winery in the afternoon was interesting. Workmen shoveled truckloads of grapes into large vats. There, with bare feet they mashed the juice into large tanks where the process of sorting, examining, and preparing it for the conversion into wine began. We saw the steps on into bottles and corks.

Our final meal consisted of clams, sole, and flan. A midnight flight landed for fuel at Santa Maria in the Azores, Bermuda, and finally Miami at 3:30 p.m. October 10.

CHAPTER 6
A DEBT REPAID TO GOD
My Spiritual Journey and Overseas Mission Trips

1965   Nigeria - my first mission experience

1967   Cataracts surgery in Pakistan

1969   My son Dudley accepts Christ after an African safari and the incredible journey to Faizabad, Afghanistan

1973   My daughter Janet in Afghanistan before the Taliban

1975   Group mission in the Dominican Republic

1977   More cataract surgery in Pakistan and trip to the kingdom of Swat

1979   Lighthouse for Christ Mission in Mombasa

The fourteen years from a freshman in college until the return of my release from the Army, I think of as my atheist years. I wasn't a thoroughgoing denier of God, just a person intent on getting an education. But, I did look askance at things like miracles, considering things like the good and bad features of the world's great religions and not giving God what we call "the time of day." But God is not called "the hound of heaven" for no reason. He continued to snap at my heels in various and consistent ways during those years.

Whereas I could have been called a non-believer in those years; starting in 1952 I entered a period of becoming a make-believer. I started going back to church for many of what are called "the wrong reasons." I wanted to be a good husband to my wife, Margaret, who was a Christian since age twelve, had grown up in a believing family, and even today affirms that God let her know that it would work out successfully to become "unequally yoked" when I had proposed marriage. I must not have been a very convincing atheist in those early years of our married life. We were wed in a Baptist church with plenty of witnesses to my declaration to cherish and honor my bride, to go through sickness and health at each other's side, and to not part until death of one or the other. Because Margaret wanted to go to church, I went too.

My mother and father were members of the Methodist church that boasted of a very popular preacher. Margaret and I decided to accompany them there. Also my mother sang in the choir, and I was proud of her and liked to hear her sing. In addition, we acquired friends among the finest families in town, and that quickly helped my practice to grow. The county agricultural agent lived across the street from my parents, and he brought his mother to me for cataract surgery, the first such operation done in Fort Lauderdale. Most residents had gone to Miami for major eye surgery prior to that time. The operation was successful and my reputation grew.

Another "excuse" for attending church was the growth of the two children God had given Margaret and me, a daughter, Janet, and a son, Dudley. I reasoned that exposure to Sunday School would be good for their development and help them become nice kids.

All these reasons for going to church are said to be superficial and wrong, but God was patiently drawing me to Himself.

In January 1959, Margaret and I went with Mother and Dad to Miami to hear a message by a famous missionary to India, Dr. E. Stanley Jones, author of a then popular book titled *Conversion*. Dr. Jones's subject was submitting one's subconscious mind to God's control. I think he was mainly saying that many Christians are willing give their conscious mind with its reasoning, decision making, and awareness to biblical principles, but their subconscious mind, their reactions to daily interruptions, are still unconverted. Many people who call themselves Christian still exhibit anger, rage, resentment, and get too easily upset. E. Stanley said that a person is not deep down converted if he or she flies into a rage over something like a spilt glass of milk. God is able to convert our reactions to moments of peace and calm if we surrender our subconscious mind to Him.

Being impressed with Dr. Jones's message, I decided to give his idea a try in my own life. I knelt at the altar and asked God to take charge of my subconscious mind, still choosing to keep my reasoning and decision making conscious mind under my personal control. The effective results were almost immediate and miraculous. A new peace and calm became characteristic of my life that also was apparent to family and friends. Being cut off in traffic on busy streets, waiting my turn to enter a main thoroughfare from a side street, being patient in check-out lines, and in numerous other ways I was changed. I had not previously been a volatile person, subject to fits of anger and outbursts, but even the suppressed forms of resentment became things of the past for me.

I didn't realize until sometime later, but another appreciated benefit of my change was that the migraine headaches I had suffered about once a month since high school days disappeared, never to trouble me again. I regret that both my children inherited migraine headaches with which they still contend.

In late February of that same year, I sat at a Methodist Men's special evangelistic meeting under the preaching of Reverend Harry Denman in West Palm Beach, and was inspired to make a total and complete surrender of my life to Jesus Christ. I became "born again," a "true believer," and changed the course of my life. I became aware that I was indebted to God for my progress through medical school, internship and residency, and I began to think about how I could repay my debt to Him. A truly special way was opened to me six years later.

My brother-in-law, James W. McCann, Jr., M. D., had finished a residency in ophthalmology in 1962 at the same place where I had trained, Grady Hospital, so I invited him to join me in my practice in Fort Lauderdale. Margaret was thrilled when Jim accepted the offer.

Jim's opportunity to do cataract surgery was slowly increasing during the first two years of private practice. In addition, he did not get to operate on as many patients as I did at The Gradies because the house staff had filled since the war, and there were more doctors to work on the same amount of patients. Jim felt he would benefit from a way to quickly gain more experience. He found the opportunity to do a great deal of eye surgery when he was offered the chance to spend one month at the eye hospital in Kano, Nigeria, as a visiting surgeon.

When Jim returned a month later, he felt more confident in his skills, but he was disturbed about something else.

"What's upsetting you, Jim," I asked.

"The missionary doctors and nurses seemed to have a peace and satisfaction about life that I don't have," he said.

A missionary named Rich Cannon was scheduled to speak at my church soon, and I suggested that Jim go with me to hear Rich. Jim learned from the talk, and later private conversation with Rich that what he lacked was a personal relationship with Jesus Christ. He, though a member of a church that had done little to inspire or encourage him, made then a genuine conversion that changed his life and values. Now we both had something in common to talk about and share.

We planned to each give one month each year, alternately, to serve in a mission hospital abroad while the other partner manned the home front. We had two stipulations. Each place had to be already doing eye work, and each had to be a true missionary facility that was preaching the true gospel of Jesus Christ. We would be helping in a small, but genuine, way to spread the Kingdom of God on earth.

The next year, 1965, I went to the eye hospital in Kano.

The large, square waiting room of the Kano Eye Hospital had every bench and chair occupied by outwardly calm patients waiting for their turns to see the visiting doctor who had come from America to restore eyesight to many of the blind residents of that area in Northern Nigeria. The middle of January offered mild, sunny weather, the most comfortable month of the entire year in that near equatorial climate, so the work was progressing smoothly and quietly. I glanced at the long list of unfamiliar names and called for the next patient to be examined.

"Mohammadoo," I drawled in my southern accent.

No response. I repeated again. Still no one moved.

The Hausa native aide who was assisting me with keeping order and translating for those who spoke no English, shouted a snappy and emphatic, "MohammaDUU!"

A tall, very dark-skinned man, clothed in blue tribal robe, roused from a light sleep, snatched the small, round cap from his head, and leaped to his feet.

A quick glance revealed his right eye to be normal, as the man pointed to his left eye and said, "I do not see with this eye."

Through a cornea that resembled frosted glass, I could see a white mass of scar tissue where the pupil and iris should have been. The globe was shrunken into a state called phthisis bulbi in ophthalmology textbooks. The eye was hopelessly and permanently blind.

After checking the vision of the good right eye and examining the interior to confirm that it was normal, I tried to explain, in simple English words, that the left eye was blind and that no operation or medicine would help. Mohammadu was having difficulty comprehending, so I asked my aide, Philip (the Christian name given him by the hospital director) to help. Philip took the man to the front door and, in a loud voice and with English words, said simply, "the doctor says your eye is spoiled."

That seemed to satisfy Mohammadu, and he went down the front steps and across the dusty front yard.

I thought about my own situation. Why was I here in a Christian mission hospital, five thousand miles from my home and family in Florida, willing to give of my time and efforts to help the dedicated permanent staff show and tell the people of this foreign land of the love of God as demonstrated by the Great Physician, Jesus Christ, when a mere twenty years before, my own spiritual eyes had been blind to the truth? My trip to Nigeria was the first of nearly a dozen similar journeys to restore vision to eyes that had not been completely "spoiled."

Every morning as I walked to the clinic building I could see a line of some two hundred patients, many having walked for days, standing and waiting to see the doctor. The mission had a policy of charging some fee, however small, to each patient. Free treatment was neither appreciated nor encouraged. Patients felt better if they had paid even the equivalent of pennies for what would be expensive surgery in America. The mornings were spent examining patients, selecting those eligible for surgery, then operating in the afternoons. With no other facilities for hundreds of miles, we had plenty of work.

Intraocular implants were not yet known, so we just removed the cloudy lenses and gave our patients thick cataract glasses which were a vast improvement over their prior condition. I was able to do fifteen or twenty surgeries each day. The blind patients often arrived holding a stick in one hand with a family member or friend holding the other end and leading the path. It was about the easiest way to guide a blind person.

The four weeks in Kano proved a rich experience and prepared me for more trips to come.

On the last day there, a telegram arrived from Florida informing that my father had died quietly in his sleep. Though the news was sad, the fact that Dad had not suffered was a blessing. We would all choose to end our life that way if we had the choice. It was already time to return home, but the trip was more sad than any I had ever made. How glad I was that Dad and I had enjoyed that wonderful safari together six years earlier.

1967

Having made contact with TEAM (The Evangelical Alliance Mission) I was scheduled to visit Bach Hospital in Abbottabad, West Pakistan, in the spring of this year to give a month of eye surgery. The doctor who had started the work at Bach Hospital several years ago was Andy Kaarsgaard, who had been forced to return to his home in Winnipeg, Canada, because of his wife, Olive's health problems. I had visited Andy last year at his home when my family was doing a trip across Canada. We spent a few hours talking about how he had managed the eye work in Pakistan, especially about the way he had performed cataract surgery. Andy showed me the technique of the Graefe knife incisions and the tumbling out of the cataractous lens by what is called the Smith-Indian method. It was fast, efficient, and would serve me well in Pakistan.

The Graefe knife has an inch long, very thin and very sharp blade on one side, and a delicate tip. When operating on the right eye, the knife tip enters the extreme margin of the cornea, known as the limbus, passes across the anterior chamber in front of the cataract and exits the opposite limbus, thus traversing the eye between the 9:30

and the 2:30 position on a clock face. The sharp edge of the blade, facing the operator sitting at the patient's head, slices upward and exits at the 12:00 o'clock position. The left hand holds the knife when operating the left eye, going from 2:30 to 9:30 o'clock. The surgeon must be equally skilled with each hand to do this type of operation.

When Margaret learned of the plans Jim and I had made for alternate year mission trips, she announced she wanted to go along and help. I was eager to agree.

Pakistan is nearly half way around the world from Fort Lauderdale, so Margaret and I planned a trip to encircle the globe with the major stop being Bach Hospital.

There was a stop-over in New York to confirm our travel plans with our agent, Mr. Paisley, and to buy new suitcases. Our old ones had broken apart on the flight from Fort Lauderdale. We had time in the afternoon to enjoy an exhibit of Andrew Wyeth paintings, one of our favorite artists.

At Orly airport outside Paris, we picked up a rental Renault and drove to Chartres to examine the famous cathedral with two unequal spires. A trip from there to Mont St. Michel was a thrilling experience. The city is cut off from the mainland at high tide, but a thin causeway allowed us to get close with our car. The cathedral and abbey at the peak of the mount must be visited on foot. Our guide spoke only French, but I was able to follow most of what he said by refreshing my freshman college study of that language. Mont St. Michel is noted for its fluffy omelettes and delicious sea food coquilles.

Driving back toward Paris along the river Loire, we visited nine different magnificent French chateaux in a three day trip. Being so early in spring, there were few American or British tourists, and the guides only lectured in French. My understanding of the language improved rapidly. We visited Brissac, Saumar, Azay le Rideau, Langeas, Chenonceaux, Ambois, Blois, Cheverny, and Chambord, the largest and grandest of all.

Flying out of Paris, we crossed the Swiss Alps before landing in Rome, Beirut, and finally Teheran. With only a casual look at one of our bags that he had asked us to open, the inspector said, "I'm sorry, but it's regulations."

To the north and west of Teheran are snow-covered mountains, but in the city the weather was mild and clear. About half the women wore shawls or veils, but half were dressed like westerners. Auto traffic was chaotic with no apparent regard for rules.

The Museum of Fine Arts illustrated the differences between Islamic and European designs. Paintings, jewelry, and carpets in oriental style contain principally geometric patterns, not often animals or figures. Tile works inside mosques were colorful and restful, pleasing to the eye.

Just outside the city where a spring bubbles into a large, clear pool beside a large rock mound is where Persians wash their carpets and place them upside down on the rock hill to dry. Even the back sides of the fifty rugs were pretty.

In the basement of a large bank are displayed the crown jewels. The value of the jewels supports more than half the nation's currency, the rest by gold bricks. The sister stone to the Kohinoor diamond, hundreds of emeralds, rubies, sapphires, and diamonds make a dazzling display. The Nadir throne is inlaid with 26,733 precious stones. The Persian crown jewels are more spectacular than either the British or the Turkish crown jewels.

A small restaurant named Sandy's features Iranian caviar. One serving for $2.25 was generous enough for both of us. A kebab of meat plus rice completed the meal.

The Blue Mosque in Isfahan had some of the most beautiful tile masonry we had ever seen. Nearby was a sports field where polo is reported to have first been played.

The next day we flew to Shiraz; from there we went by car to Persepolis, the great capitol of the Persian Empire of Cyrus, Darius and Xerxes from 500 B. C. To 350 B. C. Alexander the Great smashed the empire and burned the towns. Still standing is the great retaining wall that allowed the level area for the city. To climb the stairs to the top, we had to negotiate a series of Z-shaped switch backs. The University of Chicago had begun excavating the city in 1938. The Great Gate is decorated with figures of bulls bearing human heads. Mammoth stone carvings of various animals such as lions, horses, camels. rams, bulls, giraffes, and an antelope called the addax. The human figures of Persians had flat topped hats, and the Medes had rounded top hats.

The Persian government is trying to encourage the planting of trees in the barren plains that resulted from the senseless clearing of all trees from the Near East.

Our guide had spent six months in the United States, in Atlanta, Georgia, of all places, and had seen Stone Mountain. His English was quite good, of course.

Back in Shiraz we were disappointed that it was too early for the roses, for which the city is famous, to be in bloom, but we did visit the Pahlavi Medical School and noticed copies of Adler's Textbook of Ophthalmology and Beeson's Textbook of Medicine in English. In much of the Middle East, medicine is taught in the English language because nearly all the textbooks are in English.

Stopping at an outdoor bakery, we watched the cooking of bread in flat cakes called "naan." A wad of dough, the size of a tennis ball, is rolled out into a flat oval about one foot by two, placed on a leather pillow and slapped quickly into the curved, vaulted ceiling of the very hot oven. Three minutes later the loaf is extracted with a long metal hook. At lunch, we sent back the European bread and asked for some "naan." As we finished the meal with a small cup of real Turkish coffee, the cook seemed pleased.

From Teheran, we boarded an Afghan Airways DC-6 to fly to Kabul with a stop at Kandahar. The locals call the airline "Scariana" and say they make "three frights a week." We were made aware of the frightening situation as an automobile was loaded into the front half of the passenger section and tied down with ropes. In any rough weather, we twenty five passengers would certainly be swept out the back of the plane along with the car. In Kandahar they unloaded the car, but exchanged its place with an entire airplane engine, just as heavy, and secured just as lightly with a few ropes. We experienced two of the "frights" for the week.

The Kabul airport is at the bottom of a bowl surrounded by snow-covered mountain peaks. Planes have to descend in tight circles to land. We were met by Dr. Howard Harper, a missionary ophthalmologist with whom we had corresponded. Howard was about to give up on us because our names were not on the passenger list he was given there in Kabul, but fortunately for us, he decided to wait and see if we had arrived. Of course we were the last two through customs, all the diplomatic passports going first. Howard has been asked by the king of Afghanistan to supervise the eye work in the country, there being only thirty doctors with any training in eye diseases in the whole country of eighteen million residents.

Howard was able to show us where he worked, and I suggested we might return here on our next mission trip to offer what little help we could be in one month. One can stay in the country thirty days as a tourist and do eye surgery without a work permit.

We were driven to Howard's home to meet his wife, Monika (who had escaped the fire bombing of Dresden, Germany, at age five, by riding a freight train with her little three year old sister). The Harpers have three lovely daughters, Naomi, Faith and Joy. We all enjoyed a real Arab dinner sitting on the floor with pillows at our backs and the food served on hand decorated brass trays.

Christians are allowed in Afghanistan, but may hold services only in private homes. The next day, Sunday, the Scottish minister preached with a lilting accent to about thirty Americans and Brits, who were mostly workers on government projects.

On our way to the airport as we left, Margaret and I bought some splendid lapis lazuli jewelry. High quality lapis is mined in the northern part of the country. I also purchased a mother-of-pearl inlaid antique rifle, a muzzle loader, flint lock piece made in 1805. Not having room in the bags to fit the five foot long weapon, I boarded the plane with it slung over my shoulder and was not even questioned. Imagine trying that these days!

The air route to Pakistan took us over the famed Khyber Pass and into Peshawar, then on to Rawalpindi, later named Islamabad. Russell Irwin, husband of the missionary doctor we had come to work with, Phyliss Irwin, almost let us pass him by at the airport, as he said, "I didn't expect to meet a missionary packing a rifle."

Piling everything into a VW bus, we started for Abbottabad. The Urdu ending "abad" means the place of, or the city of. On the route we would pass Taxila, so we decided to make a stop to see Dr. Norvel Christy, a missionary eye surgeon who is extremely busy and, with one assistant, performs ninety to one hundred cataract operations each day, starting at 4:00 a.m. and finishing at 9:00 a.m. before seeing patients in the afternoon in the clinic. Norvel operated on five thousand cataracts last year.

You may ask why so many people in North Africa, the Middle East, and India have cataracts so early in life as compared to people in America and Europe. The answer seems to be a combination of multiple vitamin deficiency and exposure to intense sunlight. A doctor in North Carolina who gave his patients with early cataracts a regimen of multiple vitamins found that many were able to postpone surgery several years and some even improved. Dr. Victor Rambo, a well respected missionary eye surgeon in India for many years found that men and women who wore broad-brimmed hats developed cataracts less often than those who wore no head gear or only skull caps or wrap-around Arab type head cloths. In America we expect cataract patients to be in their seventies or more, but in India cataracts are common in those age forty or fifty.

Bach Hospital, started primarily as an eye facility by Dr. Andy Kaarsgaard, had to revert to a general type hospital after Andy and his wife, Olive, had to return to their home in Canada because of health problems. Phyliss Irwin could accomplish any type general surgery and examination on female patients because male doctors are not allowed to examine females below the neck. In preparation for my coming, Phyliss had emptied as many patients and delayed elective surgery as much as possible in order to free up enough beds for the cataract patients soon to come.

At Bach Hospital, located in the city of Mushirabad, just north of Abbottabad, Margaret and I were given a nice room and supper. Going to the clinic the next morning, I quickly adjusted to the work. One hundred patients were anxious to be seen as things got started. By the end of the day I had scheduled fifty seven patients for surgery tomorrow, some fifty cataracts and seven others. The hospital is a forty two bed facility. After the first day of surgery, the census was up to eighty. In addition to the bed patient, each needed one family member to stay beside the bed and serve as nurse and cook. The hospital does not provide food, so many families cooked small meals over little fires in the yard beside the hospital building.

All fifty seven operations were completed by early evening and was said to be the most ever done in one day at Bach Hospital.

Margaret had two jobs. On clinic days she cut centered, three inch holes in towels to make proper eye drapes and on surgery days she held the spot light to help illuminate the eyes during my surgery.

Clinic patients were seen on Mondays, Tuesdays, Thursdays, and Fridays. Surgery was Wednesday and Saturday. There were seventy to one hundred patients each clinic day and forty to sixty surgeries on operating days. The surgery room had three tables, side by side. Patients would sit on the floor near the entrance door, get their eye drops and sedation medication, then climb onto an empty table. I gave the local anesthetic to all three of the first patients of the morning or afternoon, then one injection after each case was completed before moving to the second table. Each patient had the time required for two surgeries, about fifteen minutes, for the anesthetic to have its full and desired effect before his or her operation would begin.

In the three weeks of work, we counted two hundred fifty cataract operations done and fifty other assorted cases, like eye lid eversion for trachoma, pterygiums, iridectomies, glaucoma procedures, and lacrimal operations (tear sac procedures). In addition to filling all the beds in the hospital, we pitched tents on the grounds for additional beds. At the peak day, we had one hundred forty patients under hospital care. I made rounds on the patients both inside the hospital and in the tents. We thanked God that some 92% of the cases were without complication and another 5% were at least satisfactory and improved. We did have six cataract patients who developed a serious infection which was found to be caused by a contaminated bottle of anesthetic eye drops that was used on some patients that exhibited pain during the surgery. As quickly as we found the problem, we corrected it, but the six patients finally lost most of the vision in the operated eye. How we thanked God for having given people two eyes in his wise planning.

In addition to the eye work, Margaret and I were allowed to enjoy many other pleasures of our stay in Pakistan. It was almost enough just to look out of the windows of the hospital to see the beautiful snow-covered peaks of the Hindu Kush mountains to the north. Also meeting and working with the hospital staff of nurses and helpers and sharing meals and conversations with all of them was delightful.

I also helped Phyliss with some general surgical patients such as a bowel obstruction, a ruptured appendix, a tonsillectomy, removal of an abdominal tumor, and a broken arm that has happened three years before and was extruding a segment of dead bone.

One afternoon we went by a bazaar and saw a pharmacy where any drug from Lydia Pinkham's compound to penicillin could be bought without a prescription.

That evening we were invited to the home in Abbottabad of the contractor who had built many of the hospital buildings at Bach Hospital. Russ and Phyliss brought their youngest daughter, Cindy, age five. Two other missionary couples, the Thompsons and the Pietches, joined us. Bill Pietch is an evangelist and business manager of the hospital. Karen Pietch is a nurse. Ann Thompson is the operating room supervisor and Dave Thompson, a Scotsman from Edinburgh with a strong accent, does maintenance work for the complex. We ate pilau, yellow rice, and green tea.

A late walk one afternoon through the neighboring village gave us a glimpse of country life. Some fields were being plowed by oxen and a hand controlled plow. In other fields dahl, a grazing herb was being grown, and in a great ravine, terraces for rice planting were being prepared. It was fascinating to see how otherwise useless steep mountainsides were converted into a series of small, level terraces for growing rice.

The charming English woman, Lady Noon, wife of a former Prime Minister of Pakistan, awaited our return. We found her to be entertaining and interesting, informing us about life in days of former British control.

The Irwins drove us one evening to a nearby city, Manshera, for a wedding feast. The new bride was kept in a back room. Only the women were allowed to see her. Several teenage girls could only peek at us from behind partially closed doors. Dinner was served as we sat on the rug covered floor. The typical fare was pilau and yellow rice, but we also ate small round balls of fried dough that was highly seasoned and resembled "hush puppies." Meat patties and chapatis (flat round bread) were also served. The dinner was completed with oranges and green tea.

A young surgeon named Bob Blanchard had recently come as a resident missionary to work at Bach Hospital. I gradually trained him in cataract surgery so he could continue the eye operations when needed after I left. He could send the complicated cases to Taxila. Bob learned rather quickly and was most pleasant to work with.

One Friday we returned to Abbottabad to witness a Muslim parade in which man chant, beat their bare chests with their bare hands until bloody to mourn the death of one of Mohammed's grandsons named Hussain. This Muharram, as it is called, was a stunning affair. A few men slashed their backs with chains containing small knife blades that cut into their skins and left a trail of blood in the streets. Those Muslims were serious about this practice of their faith.

Another new experience to me was a visit to a nearby mountain village where a leech doctor sold leeches, which he applied to patients not only to relieve bruises but also to treat other various illnesses. He brought out one jar with a five inch long leech swimming around in the water. We were also hosted to tea by the man who had originally helped Andy Kaarsgaard obtain the land on which Bach Hospital is built. This "high tea" consisted of cakes, biscuits, cookies, meat pies, boiled eggs, roast chicken and lots of tea. Cindy ate four of the hard boiled eggs and developed a tummy ache before we got back home. The chicken was tasty but tough, probably because it hadn't been raised in a henhouse but roamed free and had to fight off its predators.

Another afternoon an itinerant barber came to the hospital and gave me a haircut in a chair on the front porch of our house. He appreciated my payment of one rupee, about twelve cents, twice his usual fee. Margaret took the afternoon to shampoo her own hair. Afterward we visited with some of the splendid nurses like Ruth Arvidson, Marianne Sorenson, and Madeline Blanchard.

Charges to patients for services at the hospital were applied to allow patients to keep their self-esteem and help the hospital pay their own expenses. An eight day hospital stay was only charged twenty five cents, lab tests were twelve cents, and an operation only cost $1.50. Eye sutures are very expensive, but that cost was eliminated by my saving fragments left over from cataract surgery at home. Each end of the absorbable suture material has a needle attached, so they were immediately reusable. I had accumulated several pieces which we re-sterilized again for use in Pakistan. There were even a few left over for Bob to use later.

Russ and Phyliss and Cindy drove us to Rawalpindi when we finished our work and left Bach Hospital. Margaret and I told them goodbye and promised to return again if the good Lord willed. I figured I had made good on a part of my debt to God for bringing me through medical school and getting me trained as a specialist. The Irwins waved to us from the airport desk as we taxied away in the Trident jet for Karachi. We felt like we were leaving a part of our family, and perhaps they did too. I still had the Afghan gun on my shoulder when we left Rawalpindi, but on the BOAC flight from Karachi to

Bangkok, Hong Kong, and Tokyo, the captain had kept the harmless but fear provoking weapon in a forward cabinet. The Japanese in Tokyo kept the gun in a customs lock room until our departure a week later.

We were housed in the Imperial Hotel in Tokyo, the old wing being the original Frank Lloyd Wright design with rather low ceilings and colorful, angular hallways. We enjoyed the many features of one of our favorite architect's designs. We had seen his work in the buildings of Florida Southern College near home.

The first day was given over to an excursion to Hakone. Busses from three or four hotels gathered at a common location and reshuffled passengers according to language groups before proceeding on. Clouds parted about noon allowing us a clear view of Mt. Fujiyama, something that happens only twice each month except in more clear weather in January and July. The Hotel Hakone Kanko was reached by a ferry ride across a lake with a view over a beautiful green golf course in the valley below.

We relaxed in a hot sulfur springs bath that afternoon. Dressed only in kimonos and slippers provided by the hotel, we first washed our bodies with soap and rinsed using small buckets of tap water poured over ourselves before stepping into the warm pool of somewhat smelly sulfur water. A large window gave a view of a lovely small garden as we soaked in the relaxing water. When we returned to our room, two young girls gave us thorough massages, saying "I sank you," as they left. We felt the stress of the three weeks of back straining work at the operating tables in Pakistan fade away. A tempura dinner of shrimp, fish, eggplant, asparagus, pea pods, mushrooms and onion was prepared at table side by a chef who entertained us with flourishes and skillful knife handling. The meal was concluded with an orange and green tea. A stroll along the lake front as the evening closed the last glow of the afternoon sunlight completed our day.

Riding the famous bullet train from Tokyo to Kyoto the next day was exciting. Controlled by a central office in Tokyo, the one hundred-mile-an-hour train arrived exactly on time, quickly loaded, and arrived exactly on the minute in Kyoto.

After a big serving of delicious fresh strawberries the next day, a bit of chocolate was enough for lunch before we boarded the bus for an afternoon tour of Kyoto. The Sanjusangendo Buddhist temple honoring Kannon, the Goddess of Mercy, was built five hundred years ago. Before a large image of the seated goddess stand one thousand life-sized carved cypress wood images, each with ten small heads atop the regular sized one and thirty eight extra arms. . Behind all these figures are ancient carvings of the various protectors of Buddha, such as the god of thunder, the god of wind, and so forth. On opposite ends of the back wall are huge faces of fierce gods, one with open mouth saying, "aaa," the other with closed mouth saying, "mmm," the alpha and omega of the Japanese alphabet. Behind the temple is an archery range and a group of trophies are displayed on the rafters inside.

We climbed a mountain overlooking the city of Kyoto, Japan's capital from the thirteenth to mid nineteenth centuries, to see the temple of Holy Water. Pilgrims still drink from the spring now flowing down concrete troughs. The temple's large roofs are supported by small bases of intricate wood brackets. From the peak, we had a panoramic view of the city below.

On the ride down we visited a war memorial garden dedicated to the soldiers of all nations who had died in Japan in World War II plus a tomb of the unknown soldier. A huge likeness of the Goddess of Mercy, Kannon, faces the garden. A modern Shinto shrine near the bottom of the mountain was quiet, peaceful and beautiful, free of clutter and images.

The following day was a holiday, Children's Day, with all the schools closed and numerous children with their parents filling the public parks and temple areas. All were polite and orderly and many posed smiling for pictures.

We visited a Zen Buddhist garden of raked sand with a few stones placed here and there. A monk explained how the sand represents the flow of life, interrupted by troubles and problems, portrayed by the rocks. The goal of life is nirvana, a state of freedom from life's illusions and delusions and a fusing of the human spirit with the spirit of all creation. Few achieve this state, and no way is offered to overcome sin and ignorance except to try harder.

The Nijo castle has a surrounding elevated wooden walk that squeaks like the chirping of a nightingale when walked on. Its purpose was to signal the approach of intruders. Built by a shogun from Tokyo to pay his respects to the emperor in Kyoto, it contained many rooms with beautiful paintings and intricate wood carvings.

After more fresh strawberries for lunch, we were treated to a cherry blossom dance in a theater. Margaret and I were the only westerners, and the opening tea ceremony meant little to us, but was very important to the Japanese in attendance. The performance of the dance was beautifully staged and executed by a large cast of dancing girl actors. The story told of the arrival of Admiral Perry's fleet to Japan, the indecision of the Japanese people to the opening of their country to the West, the fusing of the Imperial family with the Shogunate power lords, and the final peace. The music that accompanied the play was not pleasing to our ears trained to western music.

At dinner we ate sukiyaki and got more practice with chopsticks.

Saturday was a full day tour of Nara, Japan's first capital city. A large park with hundreds of tame deer at the city's edge provided us with much fun. When the deer were offered cookies, they would nod their head two or three times in polite Japanese fashion, then accept the offering. When you wished the deer to leave, you displayed both hands empty and they would walk away quietly.

The world's largest bronze statue of Buddha sits in the world's largest wooden building in Nara. The structure is one hundred sixty feet high. The Buddha's nostrils are large enough for a child to crawl into. Huge wooden images of the "aaa" and "mmm" temple guardians are on either side of the temple gate.

After lunch we visited a Shinto shrine that is decorated with two thousand stone lanterns along the approach and one thousand brass lanterns inside the buildings. A wedding was in progress as we approached, the bride on display, unlike a Pakistani bride, was resplendent in her colorful kimono.

The Monoyama Castle is six stories high. Taking an elevator to the top, we walked down, stopping at each level to view the armor, costumes, paintings, and household items. From another shrine, dedicated to the goddess of agriculture, a path leads to the top of an adjacent hill, its way spanned by 15,000 vermillion colored torii arches. We walked the pathway a bit to get the effect, but didn't try to count the arches.

Supper was a special barbeque of beef, chicken, prawns, and delicious vegetables cooked right beside our table.

Sunday we returned to Tokyo on the bullet train, again exactly on schedule. We were housed again in the old wing of the Imperial Hotel. The room was elegant, but small by modern standards. This wing of the hotel is to be torn down next year to make way for a multi-storied addition. At supper we encountered a couple from Fort Lauderdale who own the pet store where we usually trade. We shared stories of our sightseeing with the Mr. and Mrs. Hobbs after the meal.

Monday I had planned to attend a contact lens meeting in Tokyo, but learned it had been postponed until two weeks later. Margaret and I spent the day shopping for gifts for family and friends and shipping our excess baggage home by mail.

Our final day in Japan was a trip to the city of Nikko and a Shinto shrine with painted wood carvings of the famous see no evil, hear no evil, speak no evil monkeys. The ones in Nikko are claimed to be the originals. A drive up the hairpin highway with twenty four switchbacks was dizzying, but we could see nothing because of the heavy cloud cover. There were some lovely cherry trees in bloom and an abundance of azaleas in full color at their peak.

Our last day was one of waiting for flight time. I was given back my Afghan gun at the airport, to be stored in a closet since it wouldn't fit in the overhead rack. As the plane was not full, we had room to stretch our legs and rest on the long flight back to America. Landing at Anchorage, Alaska, and again in Chicago, we arrived in Fort Lauderdale again safe and happy.

1969

As a graduation present to my son, Dudley, I offered him a dual vacation: a safari in Africa, followed by a missionary medical trip to Afghanistan. In addition to the two adventures, the trip would accomplish two other objectives of a loving father with his son: to prove whether Dudley had leanings toward medicine as a career, or if a life as a missionary might be his calling. The trip instead became an important, life changing event for him, but more of that later.

Having made all the necessary reservations and arrangements, Dudley and I left Fort Lauderdale on Sunday, June 29, and flew to New York to join the overnight flight to London.

The Protestant Chapel in the New York airport contains life size wood carvings of Christ and the twelve disciples seated at the Last Supper—a remarkable piece of art. We enjoyed having time before our departure on BOAC to view the carvings leisurely.

Once in the air, we had the luxury of a big printed menu and an elegant four course dinner, something seldom found in today's air travel. Landing in Heathrow airport, we were issued bus tickets into the city to Victoria Station and back. I called a Boy Scout leader, whom I had met in 1937 at the World Jamboree and had kept in touch ever since. Mark said he could meet us after work and ride back to Heathrow with us to see us off that evening.

Visiting the London Institute of Ophthalmology, we met Dr. Perkins who showed us some of the research work being done on monkeys. He commented that primates were hard to obtain at present because of some disease in Africa. The few monkeys housed at the Institute were enough to produce an unpleasant odor. We ate lunch in the Institute cafeteria and had a classic British steak pie.

A taxi took us to Westminster Abbey where we read the famous and familiar names on vaults and headstones in the section where important people are buried. Passing the Parliament building and Big Ben in the clock tower, we tried our skill with the Underground and correctly emerged at Hyde Park. There were no political or radical speeches in progress, but we enjoyed the fresh air and sunshine of this unusually clear day in London. Another trip on the Underground brought us to Victoria Station where we found Mark awaiting us. Britain was just changing over to a new coinage system with pence instead of shillings and pounds. Mark had a display folder illustrating and explaining the new system. We three had time for a cup of tea and some conversation before the time for our flight to be called. We told Mark goodbye and boarded the plane for Nairobi.

Making a one hour stop in Rome, the East African Airways jet was crossing the Great Rift Valley for a landing in Nairobi early the next morning. Colonel Robert Caulfeild, manager of White Hunters, Ltd., met us in the terminal and drove us in his Peugeot to the new

Hotel Intercontinental. As Dudley and I were both suffering from "jet lag," we slept most of the rest of the day, rising for a walk before dinner. I was again impressed with how suddenly afternoon turns into evening on the equator. As Dudley fell asleep that night, I stayed awake to write a letter home explaining how our son was acting very adult and how proud of him I was.

Our safari guide, Sten Cedergren, met us the next morning at the hotel. A middle-aged Swede, Sten was very fit and handsome. He introduced his wife, Lulu, a former ballet dancer, very attractive and full of sparkle. Sten served in the Ski Patrol in World War II and later came to the United States to be an instructor in the Special Forces of the Army. Sten returned to Sweden before coming to Africa to be a safari guide in 1957. We walked to the office of White Hunters, and there saw Rene (Ronnie) Babault, one of the guides who had accompanied me and my father ten years ago. Dudley and I prepared our licenses, permits, and guns in preparation for our departure the next morning. Our first camp was to be in the southeast corner of Kenya in view of Mt. Kilimanjaro just outside Tsavo National Park. The second camp would be in the Rift Valley's Loita Hills.

Sten arrived in a Toyota Land Cruiser with three African helpers, Munyoki, gun beared for Dudley and me, Mamoo, Glen's bearer and a tracker. At the city of Voi we signed in with the game ranger of the area and arranged with a local guide to meet us at our camp the next day. The tents had already been erected under lovely acacia trees by the staff of a dozen helpers. There was enough daylight remaining for us to sight in our rifles at targets before supper.

The first day was spent scouting the area. We saw several elephant, none with big tusks, several species of plains game and one lioness. The local guide we had engaged came walking into camp in the morning hours to join our men. Active hunting began the next day. I shot a bull eland, Africa's biggest antelope. We measured its horns and found they would quality for the record book. In the afternoon I shot two buffalos, one with horns big enough for the record book, a second real trophy in one day. We planned to use the buffalo carcasses for lion bait. Dudley shot a knogoni, his first trophy, and two francolin birds for supper. We saw a few more elephants, but none worth chasing. Before sundown the clouds cleared enough to give us a good view of Kilimanjaro's two peaks, Kibo and Mwengi.

As we inspected the lion bait the next day, we found no evidence that lions had been feeding. Dudley shot a steinbok, a small, tasty antelope. The cooks were preparing buffalo tail soup and sliced tongue for supper. We would eat steinbok steaks tomorrow.

There was a series of four little hills in the south end of our block. After climbing one, we saw a group of elephants walking in single file along a path. Rounding the opposite side of another hill, we were able to get in front of the elephants and view them with binoculars. The last one in line had a decent pair of tusks so Sten and Dudley moved closer to the path to await their arrival. As the final bull crossed in front, Dudley fired the .458 Winchester African rifle and made a perfect heart shot. I was taking a movie of the event and was surprised to see the beast turn and charge directly at Dudley. He calmly cranked another shell into the chamber and fired again, as did Sten with his .500 caliber rifle. The elephant crashed to the ground not fifteen paces from the pair. As the skinner and the helpers were chopping out the tusks later, Dudley asked him to save an ear for him. A year later as it hung in his den, a female guest asked what it was.

"An elephant ear," he said.

"What's it made of?" she asked.

"Elephant."

The girl fingered the ear and said, "Oh."

The movie I had taken turned out to be spectacular. As the staff was chopping out the tusks, one man noticed a festering wound in the elephant's hip where some native had shot it with a weak musket some days before. This was probably the reason the beast had charged as soon as it heard Dudley's shot. As we returned to camp, I shot a nice oryx with long straight horns. We used the body for more lion bait. Dudley shot an similar oryx the next day. We came upon three honey badgers as we drove back to camp. They ran ahead of the car for nearly half a mile before darting off into the bush.

The elephant burgers we ate for supper were made from the meat around the face, but were only average tasting and needed a lot of seasoning—not our favorite meat.

The following day it was Dudley's turn to bag a big buffalo while I filmed. On the last day in this first camp Dudley obtained a very nice kudu with small ivory tips on its double twisted horns, a nice trophy for his den. We never saw a male lion except one cub feeding with its mother on the eland carcass.

Stopping in Nairobi on our drive to the second camp, we replenished some needed supplies and drove to the edge of the eastern escarpment of the Great Rift Valley, one of the most spectacular sights in all of Africa. At this 7200 foot level, we could look across the valley fifteen hundred feet below and see Mt. Suswa and Mt. Longenot in the distance. The valley stretches away to the south as far as the eye can see.

When we reached the block assigned to us, we found the trucks had arrived a few hours earlier and camp was almost half erected. We saw very few zebras on our way in, and we soon learned the reason for that. A new game warden, an African, had sold a permit to an Indian to shoot one hundred zebras to obtain skins for his shop. The game warden had schemed to make about ten dollars on each animal shot. The Indians had shot most of the animals directly from the trucks, something not allowed for legitimate hunters.

On the second day in the new camp, I shot a bush-buck, again with record length horns. Dudley and I each collected a wildebeest to use for lion bait. The wildebeest is jokingly said to be an animal that God made from left over parts. The next day we each shot a zebra in a corner of our block where the Indians had not been. We would use them for our own rugs. This was more evidence that things are going downhill in Africa. In addition to their financial messes, there is widespread disease and misuse of many natural resources.

I had come to regard buffalo hunting as the pick of African thrills. We had licenses for six, so after Dudley had shot his one, I hunted and shot five, the most Sten ever had one client to obtain. Each one was a keen challenge and a thrill for me.

On our final safari day, Dudley and I each shot a warthog with nice tusks. As a final count, Dudley and I had each collected ten different animals, not counting the birds we shot for the cook pot. It had been a good safari, but we had yet another great adventure to look forward to, and as it happened, one unexpected important bonus to come.

On our way back to Nairobi, after the guns were packed away, we encountered not one, but two male lions quite near the road. The pair just looked at us as though they knew our hunting trip was over.

Having three days before we planned to leave Nairobi, Dudley and I had time to visit the Lighthouse for Christ Eye Center, a mission facility in Mombasa on Kenya's east coast. I had learned about the Center at a meeting of the Christian Medical Association in America. I had visited with the mission's founder and director, Dr. Bill Ghrist, and had been asked to come for a short visit to consider a month of service there in the future. The city of Mombasa is actually an island inhabited by a mixed population, part Muslim, part animist, and a few Christians. The clinic sits on a high bluff overlooking the boat harbor that is frequented by colorful Arab dhows and other commercial ships and has a busy schedule of patients and surgery.

Frequently on safari evenings in our tent, I had discussed with Dudley his Christian commitment. He knew the right answers and the plan of salvation, but kept insisting he was not quite ready to surrender his will and his life to Christ at his young age. Not that he was a bad or rebellious lad, just uncertain, probably thinking God would make him marry an ugly girl and send him off to some foreign land as a missionary. As Bill Ghrist and I were inspecting the surgery room at the clinic, Bill's wife, June, was speaking to a large group of patients in the waiting room, as was her custom. The Ghrists used this opportunity to give their Christian witness to people who came to the Center for help. Dudley had been sitting listening to June when his heart was warmed by the Holy Spirit and he told June he was ready to make his own commitment to Christ.

He joined June in a prayer for salvation. He could hardly wait to tell me the news before lunch.

A few years later, Dudley became a director on the board of the Center and has supported its work ever since. Now he was ready and anxious to go to Afghanistan.

We returned to Nairobi and were picked up by Sten and Lulu for a ride to the airport and a farewell dinner. As we arrived, we learned that Air India had rescheduled its departure two hours earlier than usual and we barely had time to board before workmen pulled the steps away from the plane. All we could manage was a wave to Sten and Lulu and thank them for the ride.

A stop in Bombay allowed time for coffee and cookies before continuing on to New Delhi in the early hours of the morning. There was about four hours wait for the connection to Kabul, Afghanistan. About noon I approached the Ariana counter and found only an agent for Indian Airways.

"I'm sorry, Sir, but Ariana has changed its schedule last month. They fly to Kabul every Wednesday instead of Thursday. You have to wait six days," he said.

The agent would exchange our tickets for a flight on Indian Airway for Sunday, still three days away. We booked a room in the Imperial Hotel, sent telegrams to our friends in Kabul and decided to make the best of the situation. We went shopping for gifts for family and friends, and enjoyed the game of bargaining for price, a game at which the Indians are masters. One item that started with an initial price of ten rupees was finally sold for less than three. We saw the same item in another shop marked at two rupees. We had only paid four cents more than we should.

Our taxi ride to the hotel had been rather round about. We learned the next day that President Nixon had arrived and many streets were blocked off for the occasion. The driver had done the best he could to go directly to the hotel.

As this was the time of the full moon, I had an idea.

"Let's take a ride to Agra and see the Taj Mahal by moonlight,"I suggested.

"Beats hanging out here,"Dudley said.

What a beautiful sight was the Taj that night. We walked around at different angles to get the full effect and even had the taxi take us again the next morning for a daytime look. Certainly the Taj Mahal is one of the most beautiful buildings in the world, not only as seen from a distance, but the intricate inlaid carving and stone work inside. We returned to Delhi and were ready for the flight to Kabul Sunday morning.

Landing in Kabul Sunday noon, we were met by Dr. Herb Friesen, a missionary ophthalmologist, after clearing customs without having a single bag opened, and taken to his home to meet his wife, Ruth, and their four sons, ages three to nine. As we ate lunch, we learned the problems facing us. First, there is a cholera epidemic in the country and everyone leaving Afghanistan must stay three days in a buffer country before traveling on. This applied even if one has had the cholera vaccine, which we had before we left home. Second and worse was that we could not participate in an eye camp in Faizabad because I was not an Afghan resident. Herb had appealed, but had no reply yet. We all prayed and turned the problems over to God.

All the mission eye work in Afghanistan is done through an organization named NOOR. The word in the Farsi language means "light," and the letters stand for National Organization for Ophthalmic Rehabilitation. Our friend Howard Harper thought of this name. With money from Germany through the Cristophal Blindenmission, a real eye hospital is being planned in Kabul, but construction has not started yet. A shipment of three enucleated eyes arrived from London, and Dr. Jock Anderson, another missionary ophthalmologist who works with Herb, planned to do three corneal transplants. Herb drove me over to watch the surgery while he appealed again to the government for our eye camp. On the way home we drove to the place where the new hospital is planned. There is also a new International Hotel under construction, scheduled for opening in six months.

Herb took Dudley and me to two identical hills that divide Kabul into an old and a new section, making the city dumbbell shaped. The Kabul River also runs through the town and between the two hills. We climbed one hill to see the cannon which someone fires at noon each day to notify the residents of the time. The "noon boom" is fired when the clock shop at its bottom registers twelve o'clock. The clock shop sets its clocks when it hears the "noon boom."

Word came from the Minister of Health that he was busy today and would consider our request tomorrow.

The next day word came from the Minister of Health that our team would be given permission to go to Faizabad, but the written permit stated no one could participate except the staff of NOOR. A personal trip by Herb to the Minister was successful, and Dudley and I were allowed to be included. Two nurses, Grace Mancey and Rosemary Weston also could be on the team. After thanking God, we took the rest of the day to pack our supplies for the trip.

Dr. Hamid, an Afghan resident training with Herb, was also included in the team going to Faizabad. He had told us that the trip would be very interesting if we survived the "incredible journey" required to reach our destination. The trip was indeed "incredible," more than we could have imagined.

The first two hundred miles of road was paved a few years ago by the Russians. It led into the mountains toward Kunduz and was a popular route, crowded with pedestrians, horse carts, goats, children playing on the road, and broken down cars and trucks left abandoned on the road or pushed slightly to the side. Travel had to be slow because of all the obstacles to avoid and the living creatures to spare. The mountains rose starkly up, devoid of trees or shrubs. When we reached 11,000 feet, we approached what appeared to be a dead end, but the road became a tunnel piercing the final mountain peak. It must have been an engineering feat to construct. The road opened out into a more gently sloping valley that made driving easier. By suppertime we had reached a village with a tea shop where we stopped to eat. The long narrow room contained a table about six by fifteen feet, waist high. Taking off our shoes, we all climbed up to sit on the table with our backs to the wall, legs crossed in a position not very comfortable for Americans.

The waiter, serving from the opposite of the table, gave us in turn a cake of soap, an empty bowl, then rinsed our washed hands with water poured from a pitcher held over the bowl. Drying our hands by rubbing them together and waving them in the air, we were ready for the meal: lamb and rice pilau with raisins, seasoning, and naan (flat bread). Each person was given an empty glass, and one bowl of sugar with one spoon was started at one end of the table. Each person put three teaspoonfuls of sugar into the glass and the glass was filled with hot tea carefully so as not to stir up all the sugar. Only enough sugar dissolved to sweeten the first glass full. Two more servings of tea dissolved all the sugar and lasted through the meal. We had an interested group of spectators as another table of locals came into the restaurant to eat. The bill for the six dinners was just under one dollar American.

Reaching Kunduz about midnight, we found the Rest House to be filled, but we were offered the second floor lobby with sofas, chairs and cushions plus a separate bathroom for the night. We all found some way to get comfortable and slept soundly.

Having slept in our clothes, we were ready early to travel the next morning. Tea and naan for breakfast, fresh gas for the two land rovers, we faced only dirt roads from Kunduz to Faizabad, one hundred sixty miles to the northeast. When we stopped for lunch, we had an audience of children, just standing and watching. Strangers were a rare sight for them.

Dr. Hamid then said, "We'd better push on. The road ahead gets much worse." How true his words were. We forded rivers, crossed muddy and rocky flats, and drove on narrow mountain sides, only one lane wide, so that when meeting a car or truck coming from the opposite direction, one had to back up to a passing spot, a wide place made for that purpose where two cars could pass. We were grateful that we encountered very little traffic.

In a village near our destination, we stopped for tea. Seventeen men, road workers, gathered around to watch us. Learning we were eye doctors, they all presented themselves for examination. Ten had obvious external eye disease, such as trachoma, corneal opacities, and small pox scars. Three had one blind eye. The harsh sandy environment was devastating to people with no medical eye care available anywhere.

Being flagged to a stop near a Ford that had broken down by the road, we were asked by the driver who spoke some English to take one of his two boys into Faizabad to get help sent out to them. It was completely dark when we crossed the cement spillway six inches below the surface of the Faizabad River that flowed beside the town.

There were plenty of rooms available in the riverside hotel which we called the "Faizabad Hilton," and we moved in, two to a room, Herb and Dr. Hamid, Dudley and I, Rosemary and Grace. The long narrow building had a central corridor of hard packed earth with rooms on either side. The toilet was on the water side with a metal trough extending out over the water's edge with a bucket of river water to rinse refuse out into the rushing stream. One 55 gallon drum with a spigot at the bottom served for hand washing. A cement drain in the center of the floor received the dirty water. One large room near the entrance with a rug on the floor was considered the dining room where tea was served while food brought in by the guests was eaten. Each guest room had two beds, one small table, and a kerosene lamp to use at night. The rate was reasonable, about seventy cents per night per room.

Our first call the next morning was to check in with the local governor. A dozen other men squatted on the office floor, but we were ushered into the official's inner office and given chairs. Our reception was cordial, and after a proper welcome, we were sent to the local hospital. Recently built and rather large, it is only half used because of insufficient funding, but ready for future growth. We were given adequate space in the unoccupied half. The afternoon was spent preparing for our work. This included buying wire screen to cover the one window in the surgery room and installing a hinge and lock on the clinic door to insure the safety of our supplies and equipment.

We found a nice restaurant for a kebab lunch of lamb and vegetables served on metal skewers, eaten with pieces of naan, and washed down with cups of hot tea. The teapot and cups were examples of native ingenuity, having been broken and repaired with wire and cement—but leak proof. These scarce items were kept in service as long as possible.

In the late afternoon, Herb, Dudley and I went for a swim in the river where a wide place formed a nice quiet pool. We inflated an inner tube to use for floatation and play, although we couldn't stay long in the cold water that had come down from melting snow on the mountain peaks above the city.

Just before supper, an American Peace Corp doctor, his wife, and three daughters arrived at the end of a three week hike from Kabul over the mountains. Dr. Franz was teaching at Afghanistan's only medical school at Jalalabad. Their home is Monroe, Wisconsin. They had back packs and loads on two donkeys and had made the strenuous hike during a school vacation.

We enjoyed visiting with the Franz family at our shared dinner. They had crossed glaciers and mountain peaks 14,000 feet high with no mishaps or serious problems. It was an experience of which the girls will tell for years to come.

Our work started slowly with only twenty clinic patients the first day. Most had complications of trachoma and two needed lid surgery. Finishing early, we started the trachoma screening of the school children, part of the NOOR work we had agreed to do. At the girl's school (this was before the Taliban had stopped female education), the students were dressed alike in uniforms of white pants, black tops, and white head scarves. Many of the girls were very pretty and had not yet suffered the ravages of premature aging so common to Afghan women who have no access to cosmetics or beauty care and have to live a difficult and suppressed life under male domination. Seventeen of the fifty seven children had early trachoma and were given sulfa pills that had been provided by the government.

Dr. Hamid and I did the eyelid surgery in the afternoon while Herb surveyed more school children, finding the same incidence of trachoma we had discovered in the morning hours. Dudley had not shown much interest in the medical aspects of the work, but was more interested in repairing fan belts on the cars, keeping the generator functioning and other mechanical jobs for which everyone was grateful. Dudley had worked two summers in a boat yard and could take apart and repair outboard motors and fix many parts of automobile engines. He later went into engineering as a life work.

Clinic work increased the next day and each that followed, with a greater variety of pathology turning up. By the end of the week we were seeing about sixty patients in the clinic and performing about twenty surgeries each day. Our operations were very successful, with a minimum of complications. We almost had a disaster one day. When we made rounds on the post op cataract patients we found all the men kneeling on the floor and bowing their heads in prayer. One patient was a Muslim mullah, a holy man, and felt called on the lead in group prayer and worship. We stopped them before any had ruptured their eye incisions by reminding them that the Koran allowed men to pray while lying on their back in cases of illness or injury.

Two mornings I saw caravans of migrant families moving south from the approaching winter along the highway across the river. A long line of camels, horses, cattle, sheep, goats and people walking made a picturesque scene like we read of in Bible times. From Faizabad the road leads north and east into China and travelers often ride yaks along the narrow trail.

Dudley drove the Franz family to the airport for the flight back to Kabul. He was expecting to pick up Grace's husband, Gordon, but he was not on the incoming plane. On his trips to the airport, and sometimes waiting for the irregular arrivals, Dudley had made friends of the airport personnel and some of the pilots. Gordon did arrive the next day, but riding in a truck, having caught a ride for two days in jeeps and trucks coming to Faizabad.

One evening at supper time we saw four truckloads of men driving out of town with much chanting, singing and clapping. They were having a wedding celebration and they were going to fetch the bride. The wedding party returned and drove somewhere into town. We walked into town to find the group and join in the fun. We located everyone on a flat roof top, where we were ushered up and seated in choice seats. The entire party was men only and they were serving pilau, tea and a candy called "knuckle," almonds covered with solidified white sugar. An orchestra appeared and a man dressed as a woman, complete with rouge, lipstick, a veil over his head and bells on his ankles, did a dance like a whirling dervish. As the party seemed destined to continue well into the night, we left for bed.

Herb flew back to Kabul and was replaced by Dr. Murray McGavin, who planned to stay for another week to take care of the patients whom we were leaving after cataract surgery. Our last day of surgery had gone until 8:15 at night. The patients were all amazed and commented on how much it was appreciated, because the Afghan doctors never worked after 5 p.m., even for emergencies.

We averted a big ruckus at the hospital when the administration presented us with a written list of complaints, which included: putting too many patients in one room, patients getting the walls dirty and chipping the plaster, allowing patients and family sleeping in the corridors, collecting fees from patients ($2 of $3 per case), leaving trash on the floors and using outdated medicines. This last complaint, we denied and showed them the boxes and bottles with current dates printed thereon. Rather than arguing the various points in their complaint, we offered to pay for repairing and repainting the walls and having the rooms cleaned. We could appreciate the feelings of the officials who were somewhat embarrassed that their own country couldn't provide their peoples' needs and that helpers from other countries had to come and offer to help. Some of the complaints had reached the attention of the patients, and one elderly Hadji (a religious leader) told the hospital director in a loud voice that the hospital belonged to the people and these good eye doctors had come a long way to help the local residents. Our Christian world view is so different from what is found in other parts of the world.

Dr. McGavin arrived on the daily flight along with two young men from California who had obtained the very hard to acquire and very expensive ($6000) licenses to hunt Marco Polo sheep in the area. The sheep is considered a rare and desirable trophy.

Dudley and I flew back to Kabul the next day on the small plane which dared not fly high enough to require oxygen by cruising between the highest mountain peaks at wing level.

We thanked God that the cholera quarantine had been lifted and we could return straight home. We left by way of Kandahar, Teheran and Beirut, where we had an overnight in a hotel. The next day we stopped in Rome and Paris and were delayed in New York so long that we missed the scheduled flight to Fort Lauderdale. Another flight to Miami was leaving three hours later. We telephoned our family and Margaret and Janet met us there at 4 a.m. to drive us home, asking more questions than we could answer in the next week.

This trip had been a life-changing experience for Dudley and one both of us would remember the rest of our lives.

1973

This year was the time for Margaret and me to take our daughter, Janet, on a medical mission trip. She had just graduated from college and had not started a job, so she was free to go with us. Like we had done for Dudley, we wanted to expose her to medical work and the missionary life.

It was early Spring as the three of us flew from Fort Lauderdale to New York and London, where we met up with Dr. Al Smith, an ophthalmologist from Miami, and his wife, Libby. They had heard about our previous trips to Pakistan and Afghanistan and desired to join us on such and enterprise and adventure. We five boarded the Ariana jet, which landed in Frankfurt, Istanbul, and Damascus before circling down into the saucer shaped airport in Kabul, Afghanistan. As usual we were the last ones through customs, having to explain the various surgical items in our luggage.

Dr. Herb Friesen, our missionary friend who had taken care of Dudley and me four years earlier, met us with a Toyota van and took us to the International Afghan Mission guest house, where we unpacked and rested, sleeping off and on all afternoon. Herb fetched us again for supper at his home. Ruth, his wife, now has five boys and a baby girl; she only had four boys in 1969, but had since added the new boy and the very new baby girl since. They are a fine and active family, growing and adapting to a difficult and harsh environment.

Bright and early the next morning, Carol Erb, secretary of the new NOOR Eye Hospital, a million dollar facility built by the Germans, gathered us for a trip to the new building. The clinic area was especially designed for the new residency training program which had just begun. Herb had saved several patients with rare and strange diseases for me and Al to examine. We helped with the other clinic patients while the girls inspected the hospital record room where the charts from the old hospital needed sorting and filing in useable order. They would work on that later.

Herb then drove us for a look at the city. The tomb of the former king, the present king's father, was built on a hill that offered a nice panorama of Kabul. The main shopping stores face Chicken Street, a colorful place where some of the American and European hippies hang out.

Monika Harper, wife of Howard, who is in Herat on the western edge of Afghanistan doing trachoma work, joined us for supper. We spent the evening learning farsi phrases that would prove useful, such as, "look up," "look down," "look straight ahead."

Al and I spent a busy day at the hospital, that began with a prayer meeting. We saw clinic and ward patients, lectured to the residents, and consulted on a few puzzling cases. We learned the names and faces of the six residents and one girl medical student from England. Al learned how to do the lid operation for trachoma, a disease with which he had no prior experience.

Margaret, Janet, and Libby remained at the Guest House doing laundry and visiting with Ruth and the children. In the afternoon, they started working on the 13,000 charts that needed to be cross indexed and filed accurately, a job that extended several days.

Al helped in the clinic, while I worked with Herb in surgery. When we finished, we examined the newly admitted patients and found some with mistaken diagnoses. The residents pretended to know more than they really did. Our main job appeared to be improving the teaching of the resident physicians.

We five Americans enjoyed a dinner at the new Intercontinental Hotel, from which we could see the city lights below that sparkled like a sequined cloth between the mountains.

We couldn't believe they offered baked Alaska for dessert.

The next morning we encountered our friend, Raymond Knighton, director of Medical Assistance Programs, who had arrived from Chicago to convince the government officials to keep NOOR work functioning in the country. Raymond travels to many countries helping medical work in many ways and sending vast amounts of pharmaceuticals to missions. He joined us at the mission headquarters for a prayer meeting. We learned that afternoon that Raymond had convinced the government to cancel their plans for dismissing the entire forty five M. A. P. and NOOR personnel from Afghanistan.

Later in the morning, we all joined several others on a bus trip to the village of Estalif, where some lovely blue pottery is made. Wild tulips grew abundantly on the mountainsides. Janet developed stomach cramps on the bus ride, and Margaret was attacked by the same trouble the next morning. Al and I were already struggling with the same problem, which is called the "Kabul trots."

Janet took the next couple of days off to go with a group of young people to Mazar-I-Sharif in the north of the country to watch a game of bushkashi, played like polo on horses but using a dead goat as the "ball," carried against considerable opposition by one team to the opposite goal line. Janet owns her own horse at home and is a skillful rider. She really enjoyed the game. The bus drove to the nearby Russian border to look over. They were not fired on from the machine gun towers, thank God.

Sunday was the day for church, which had to be conducted in the home of the pastor. The Reverend Christy Wilson, whom Margaret and I had met before when we passed through Afghanistan, had been expelled two weeks ago. A couple of guards with rifles over their shoulders stood outside the house to insure that no Afghans attended the service. The newly built Community Christian Church of Kabul, with beautiful marble floor and graceful woodwork, was never permitted to hold a service, and was completely torn down later that year. It was sad to see such waste.

Howard Harper had returned from Herat and invited us all over for lunch with Monika and their three lovely daughters, Naomi, Faith, and Joy. One Afghan girl brought her blind sister over for tea after the meal. We learned that the government had closed the School for the Blind just three weeks ago because some of the blind children had become Christians, the excuse the authorities gave was that the money spent for the school could be better used in other ways. The girls had been taught to make baskets and brooms to sell, but now they had nothing to do.

In the late afternoon we were driven to the village of Paghman. There were some nice gardens, lacy summer homes and a little snow in shady spots. It looked like a scene form the movie Dr. Zhivago. A bread maker in one street gave us two fresh loaves from his oven, refusing pay because he said we were "his guests."

The next four days Al, Herb, and I examined many clinic patients, did several operations, and gave some lectures to the residents. Our wives and Janet continued to work on the hospital charts.

On Friday we obtained a rental car from Hertz, a Toyota sedan, one of only two on the lot, and loaded it with food, extra clothing and supplies for a trip to the main tourist attraction in Afghanistan, the city of Bamiyan. Howard and Monika, their three daughters, and a medical student from England, John Gilbert, rode in his Land Rover. The paved road was fine as far as Charikar, but we had to turn onto a dirt trail at the 73 km. Marker. As we rolled into the first village, a group of boys ran along side the Toyota yelling, "Mistah, Punchah." The left front tire had leaked around the valve, so we tightened the valve, pumped up the tire and continued on. The road was bumpy, curvy, muddy, rocky, and narrow, requiring strenuous and careful driving. We traveled beautiful valleys and a rushing river for miles. In another village we again heard, "Mistah, Punchah." one rear tire had a genuine puncture and had to be changed. The spare tire also had a slow leak in the valve and both front and rear tires had to be pumped periodically. When we reached 10,000 feet in the mountains, Al and I had to take turns pumping as the exertion winded us each quickly.

Several small streams crossed the road to join the main river. There was one bridge, some culverts but most were just shallow ditches, although one was deep enough to get water into the trunk of the car. There were orchards of apricots, cherries and almonds, the trees in full bloom and beautiful. The surrounding mountain sides were very colorful in a variety of hues, and always in the distance rose snow covered peaks.

About sixty five miles from the pavement, the valley ended and we started on switch backs that our Toyota strained seriously in reaching the top of the Shibar Pass. In another twenty miles we reached the Bamiyan valley, one side of which was a vertical cliff of red sandstone. Into it were carved several statues of Buddha and many caves that served as shrines or homes for monks. The largest standing Buddhas, which dated from the fourth century and represented the most western spread of the faith, had all the faces and hands chipped off by Muslim authorities. On the top of the mount opposite the cliffs stood the Bamiyan Hotel. There were no rooms available in the main building, but we were given three round wood and rug huts, called yurts. Each had a proper bathroom with a marble floor, a round hole at the top and a foot high gap at the bottom for circulation. One Sears kerosene heater offered a little warmth against the frigid thirty two degree weather. We each had three heavy wool blankets with Ariana Airlines name printed on them.

A light snow fell during the night, but only stuck on the north side of the plowed fields and hills, making a beautiful and interesting picture. Our Toyota had two flat tires and a flat spare the next morning. We took off the wheels and found a tire repair shop in town for repairs.

Standing at the base of the largest Buddha statue we looked up to the top of his head one hundred seventy five feet high. A guide said we could go there, so he led Howard, Al and me up the side of the cliff, through a small tunnel and out onto the hair bun. There was no guard rail or indeed not even a wire around the edge. The view down was rather scary. A few fresco paintings adorned the cupola over the head. Margaret said she had remained below to "notify the nearest of kin" if any of us had fallen off.

Years later, when the Taliban had gained control of the country, they decided the statues were indeed religious symbols, so they hauled cannons up to Bamiyan and blasted the marvelous works of art into piles of rubble. I was glad we had seen them when they were nearly whole.

Retrieving our three wheels for the Toyota, we all drove ten miles along the valley to the Red City, a fair sized city sacked in 1222 A. D. by Ghengis Khan, who slaughtered all the inhabitants. The Harper girls found some fragments of pottery in the ruins.

Returning by the same route back, we were surprised when the Toyota started sagging in the back right side. We had broken a spring and could go no farther. God didn't even give us time to agonize over our dilemma. A chauffeur driven Land Cruiser owned by Hertz came soon behind us on the road, parked our car in a yard and asked the owner to watch it. They would send for the car later. We all piled into Howard's cruiser and returned safely back to Kabul.

Back in Kabul, Al and I resumed our work examining clinic patients and performing surgery. The girls were completing their chart filing and even started collecting statistics on certain operations and treatments Herb wanted to analyze. Al and I presented a talk at the Kabul Medical Society, showing slides and discussing the eye manifestations of internal disease.

After obtaining a new car from Hertz, I was driving, Janet in the front seat and Margaret and Libby in the back seat, when I stopped at one of the only two traffic lights in Kabul. I noticed an Afghan man pulling up beside us. He said in English, "I'll give you three camels, two horses, and twelve sheep for that young wife of yours in the front seat."

Janet screamed, "Dad, don't you dare!" as she scrunched down almost under the dash. Margaret and Libby laughed as the man sped away when I shook my head to indicate no.

That afternoon Herb, Al, and I went to the Kabul Golf and Country Club to play golf—another reminder of the British occupation days. The "greens" were round areas of firm, slightly oiled sand. After each group finished putting—that being nice because the ball always broke toward the cup, which was the lowest place in the center of the "green"—two caddies would drag an oriental carpet in an expanding circle to erase the footprints and ball tracks. The golf course was not crowded, and we had a good time.

As a special treat, we were all invited to dinner at the home of General Omar, chief of protocol for His Majesty King Sahir Khan. There were nice rugs on the floor, but very ordinary furniture for such a high government official. The food was very tasty, but our conversation was somewhat limited because of everything having to be translated into farsi and back to English.

The following day was Good Friday. We met the U. S. Air Attache to Afghanistan, Colonel Weston, and he offered to ship home any overweight baggage we had accumulated. God is still looking out for us on this trip.

We took two cars for a drive along the Kabul River east to the city of Jalalabad, nearly one mile lower in altitude than Kabul. The road, nicely paved, dips down a steep and rocky gorge. As the river tumbles down, the road curves back and forth in dizzying switch backs. Two hydroelectric dams interrupt the flow. At the first dam is a small lake and a fertile green valley. After the second dam, the water becomes a milky blue, the mud having settled in the lake above the dam, as it rushes down the steep gorge into a flat plain.

Jalalabad isn't much of a city, but is important because it is the last stop before the famed Khyber Pass into Pakistan. Lunch was fun in a sidewalk café because the waiter ran back and forth between three restaurants to obtain parts of our meal, like tea and dessert. On our drive back to Kabul we stopped to look closely at a poppy field. The opium was oozing out of the pods. We wondered if any of it would end up as heroin in America.

Al and Libby were great companions on this trip. Al, a specialist interested in children, is an even tempered, considerate person, relaxing to be with and a smart, hard worker. Libby Smith is a delightful conversationalist with a very broad Southern accent. She had a quick wit, an upbeat personality, and is an innovative worker. Libby took the lead in organizing the hospital charts in Kabul. Margaret and I enjoyed Al and Libby so much, we decided that we'd like to have them accompany us on another trip in the future.

Al and Libby flew on home from Frankfurt while we picked up a car to drive into Switzerland. Janet had shown some interest in medicine on this trip, but she also had a leaning toward theology. So I thought she would be excited that we were going to pay a visit to our dear friends Dr. Francis and Edith Schaeffer at the L'Abri teaching and learning center in Huemoz. We drove south through Germany and into Switzerland where we took rooms at the hotel in Chesieres. Snow covered the town and the mountains about, but the wind was not blowing and the sky was clear. As we were eating supper, Christian friends from home, John and Lorraine Morris walked in. They had arrived two days earlier and had attended Easter services in the chapel at L'Abri. They had learned of Dr. Schaeffer's work from a mutual friend, Boyd Anderson, who had introduced us to Fran and Edith a few years earlier. As John and Lorraine headed home the next day, we joined about one hundred young people to hear a lecture by John Sandry, husband of the Schaeffer's oldest daughter, Priscilla. Susan, the middle daughter, had married Ranald McCaulay, a teacher and lecturer to L'Abri students, and Debbie, the youngest and most vivacious daughter, had wed a brilliant German, Udo Middleman, who came once to Fort Lauderdale to speak at a church gathering, but his German accent and complicated theology left about half the lethargic church members wondering what he had said.

Youth, in search of meaning in their lives, are attracted to L'Abri where they have their "honest questions" given "honest answers," listen to audio tapes, read Dr. Schaeffer's books, *The God Who Is There, Escape From Reason, and True Spirituality.* Many become Christians, or if they already believe, have their faith strengthened.

Supper was served at the Schaeffers' home, a four story chalet, with Dr. Schaeffer at the head of the table. A few other guests had joined us, a chaplain, a missionary, and archeologist, and a book seller from India. The conversation was varied and interesting. Margaret and Janet and the archeologist's wife washed the dishes afterward while I talked further with Fran. Franky and Genie Schaeffer lived in the basement of the chalet, and Franky had begun filming the movie about Fran's book, *How Should We Then Live.*

The next morning Margaret, Janet, and I had tea with Os Guinness and his wife, Ginny. Os had written a book, *The Dust of Death,* much of which was focused upon Afghanistan and the hippies, so he enjoyed talking about our experiences in that strange land. Os later moved to the States and authored several incisive books about the Christian faith.

Dr. Schaeffer led a discussion group in the L'Abri chapel and answered all sorts of questions while sitting on the hearth in his knickers and sweat shirt. For several years we had close contact with the Schaeffers as they came to south Florida for short vacations. We would meet Fran and Edith at the Miami airport, drive them to the Florida Keys and put them aboard a private yacht for a week of relaxing pleasure cruising in the calm waters of the islands. We also had them to dinner in our home to visit with Janet and Dudley before returning them to the airport. We saw them twice more at the showing of the film *How Should We Then Live* in Atlanta, and *Whatever Happened to the Human Race* in Tampa, when we had them over to Fort Lauderdale to examine their eyes and give them new reading glasses. Margaret and I treasured our friendship with Fran and Edith and stayed in contact with Edith after Fran's death.

Fran taught me a concept that subsequently influenced my thinking about people. He regarded every individual he encountered as a person made in the image of God. That image may be clean and clear, dirty and soiled, or even badly damaged or spoiled, but an image of eternal significance to God as long as that person is capable of being brought into the kingdom of God. I have tried to remember that lesson with patients, friends or casual acquaintances, not always successfully, but seriously.

Leaving Huemoz the next day we drove through the beautiful alps to the medieval city of Gruyere, where we had to park outside the city and walk into town. We obtained a room in the Hotel St. Georges and made a tour of the castle, which had no heat and felt extremely cold to us Floridians. A hot fondue dinner helped warm us up later. It should have been good since the cheese made in Gruyere is the main ingredient.

Back in Frankfurt, we boarded a 747 for a smooth ride to New York. The tour through customs was extremely slow, causing us to miss our flight to Fort Lauderdale. In three hours we got aboard a different plane and were put in first class because of the delay, so our trip ended in real comfort, an experience quite varied and unforgettable.

1975

I had been a member of the Christian Medical Society (now called the Christian Medical and Dental Association) for as long as I can remember, but had never been on one of their frequent group missions. Margaret and I felt this year would be an appropriate time to join the team going to the Dominican Republic for an eye project at La Posada in June, not the most comfortable time of the year, but at least during the summer vacation period when the time off was easier for some of the team.

The optician who worked for me, Charles Johnson, had tried to go on a prior trip, but had it canceled because of political unrest in the region, so he was happy for the opportunity to join Margaret and me on this mission.

It's only a short flight from Miami to Hispaniola, the Caribbean island made up of Haiti on the west and the Dominican Republic on the east. Most of the other passengers on the 727 flying that day were Latins returning home or visiting relatives. They rushed aboard with hand luggage enough to fill the overhead racks and all the available cabin space with bags, sacks, stuffed animals, and flower arrangements, an unnecessary thing because flowers are more abundant on the island than in Miami. The only three seats together were in the last row, which couldn't be tilted back, but it didn't matter since the flight was only two hours long.

In the Santo Domingo airport we were met by the team coordinator, John Shannon, issued name tags, met several other volunteers, and awaited flights from other cities that were to arrive soon. The team finally consisted of five ophthalmologists, one new graduate from medical school who was planning a eye residency, nine optometrists and two optometric students, three opticians and one apprentice, eight nurses and twelve wives and three teenaged helpers. Team members had come from as far north as Canada, as far west as Oregon, as close as Florida, but mostly from the upper east of the States.

All our bags were loaded into a truck while the team members climbed into four ancient vehicles to travel the forty hot, dusty miles to the city of Nigua, meaning flea in Spanish, and the seaside resort of La Posada, a restored villa once owned by the former dictator Trujillo. The ocean breeze was delightful and the adjacent swimming pool inviting. The second storey was a large dormitory and a second building contained rooms for married couples. The evening brought coolness on the breeze and the gentle pounding of the nearby surf was a great aid to sleep after a tiring day.

The first morning, after a time of devotions, the team was told the routine for the work and had time to get a bit acquainted. We inspected the work area. Patients would come to a large examination area with two slightly darkened rooms for refractions and fundus exams. Surgery would be done at the hospital in nearby San Cristobal. We arranged our exam equipment, cleaned our refraction lenses and sorted the thousands of donated eye glasses that had already been labeled by prescription.

Most of the team visited a Pentecostal church in a nearby village that second evening. Although we nearly outnumbered the local members, we were no match for their enthusiasm in hand clapping, foot stomping, amens, and shouts of "gloria a Dios" (glory to God). The message in Spanish helped tune my ears to the language I have studied since moving to South Florida where I have to use it often.

On Monday morning the patients started arriving at dawn. When the admissions desk closed at 2:00 p.m., some four hundred thirty had passed the screening desk. Our routine was to have the patients sorted by an ophthalmologist into four categories. Category 1 were those who had no obvious eye problem, a minor superficial irritation or allergy. These were refunded their 25 cents entrance fee and sent home. They were free to purchase sunglasses if they wished. Category 2 was for patients over the age of forty with good distance vision, needing only help for reading or sewing. We had hundreds of plus power reading glasses for them to choose from the weakest plus 1.00 to the strongest plus 3.00 in a variety of sizes and shapes. The doctors' wives and teenagers were able to help the overwhelmed opticians select the most appropriate glasses for these patients. Category 3 were patients with decreased visual acuity and no obvious disease. These were ushered into the first large dimmed room with four parallel refracting lanes to be examined by four of the optometrists who rotated turns. Some jokingly commented that they worked so hard the handles of their retinoscopes got too hot to hold. Category 4 were patients with some eye problem that needed further ophthalmic consultation. In the second room they could have their eyes dilated, pressures measured and fundi inspected.

The ophthalmologists beside mewere Dr. Alan Rich from Lakeland, Florida, Dr. Harry Lawrence from Chattanooga, Dr. Duane Diller from Portland, Oregon, and Dr. John Gooch from New Orleans, whose wife and her family owned the famous restaurant Gallitoir's in the Mardi Gras city. We all took turns in the clinic and at the hospital.

With only three opticians and one apprentice, Charlie had adjusted so many glasses that his arms hung down in exhaustion at the end of the day. He couldn't decide whether to swim in the pool of take a shower and ended by doing neither. He was somewhat revived by supper and a short walk on the beach.

Most of our surgery was performed in a huge air conditioned van, sixty by eleven feet, pulled by a truck with an extra generator motor for power. The complete unit, costing $64,000 was donated by a very generous Texan, and has been very much used since given four years ago. The 140 bed hospital in San Cristobal is clean, airy and awaited our surgical patients that were soon to come.

Up the mountain from the hospital is a four storey mansion built by Trujillo, but never used because it had no electricity nor water. Today it is used as a nice cool place for picnics and a view of the valley below.

The patients increased each day from 400 to 600 to 700 and topped at 945 by the end of the week, setting a new record for the clinic. We really needed the nearby beach area where Trujillo had constructed a cement retaining wall with windows to allow the surf to splash through and form a round shallow pool that was safe and comfortable for swimming or lounging. Poor Charlie worked so hard he couldn't eat the third evening after hanging glasses on 400 noses that one day.

To do surgery on children, we had the help of a Dominican anesthesiologist named Dr. Diaz. He gave the kids ketamine intravenously which worked quite well. Mary Hawkins, the recent graduate from medical school in New York, learned to do eye surgery by helping me with making the conjunctival flaps for cataracts and placing some of the sutures after removal of the lens and copying my muscle operations for crossed eyes. Mary did one complete cataract operation on a woman whose vision was impaired by previously untreated glaucoma.

On the way back to La Posada from the hospital we found an ice cream plant and were able to buy cones. The facility was run by Jesuit priests and made high quality ice cream.

The Bible study hour in the evenings was interesting because of the varied backgrounds of the team as several new thoughts on different subjects were introduced.

Friday night after all the optometrists had returned to Santo Domingo to depart for home, the rest of us went into the city to the Cave restaurant for dinner. The Cave is a natural grotto decorated like a real limestone cavern. The food was delicious and was accompanied by music played by a dance band. Some of us took a turn at the dancing as we dined.

Saturday was a day at leisure and Margaret and I enjoyed visiting with Dr. Gooch and Alan and Linda Rich as they told of their mission trips to Africa and the Middle East. On Sunday what remained of the team split up to attend three different churches in Santa Domingo. On talking to the organist at the Baptist church, Margaret found that Mary Frances had trained as an R.N. in Columbus, Georgia, at the same time Margaret was doing a summer dietetic job there. The two girls had even double dated once. What a small world we really live in.

Having sorted out and selected the surgical cases in the prior week, the next week was given over to doing the cases. We ophthalmologists planned our schedule that Sunday evening for the week ahead. The assorted surgeries were done each day as we took turns operating and assisting.

In mid week we went into Santo Domingo for dinner in one of the city's best restaurants in the Hotel Linas. Margaret and I ate escargots, Caesar salad, and a seafood casserole, all very delicious.

Very early Thursday several of us decided to walk the eight miles to San Cristobal. We saw many aspects of village life as people were doing their morning chores. Many waved and greeted us on our way. The vans caught up with us and drove us the last mile to the hospital.

Margaret and two of the nurses went to an orphanage in San Cristobal to check the visual acuity of the nearly one hundred children, ages five to nineteen, who reside there. Only a few had vision problems, and they were told to go the next eye project to be held at La Posada.

Dr. Diller and I examined the eighty post op patients while the other surgeons did new cases that required no follow up. When we fitted the cataract patients with the strong glasses, they showed great excitement at their new vision. Some of the patients brought us fruit, nuts and vegetables to express their appreciation.

On the day before departure, John took us to the cathedral where Christopher Columbus is buried. We bought souvenirs of sandals, belts and amber—the Dominican Republic being, along with Russia, one of the richest sources of amber in the world.

Our final evaluation of the two weeks revealed we had screened 3000 patients, given 1400 reading glasses, 650 prescription glasses, 500 sun glasses and done 121 operations. Dr. Lawrence's oldest son, Robbie, age sixteen, asked and received permission to remain at La Posada all summer to help. Harry and Sue promised to send more clothes from Chattanooga as soon as they returned home.

Margaret and I returned to Miami Saturday morning, pleased to have been part of the group of such pleasant, cohesive and dedicated Christian workers, serving the Lord with our individual, God-given talents. Christian harmony is a wonderful thing to behold.

1977

The time approached for another trip to Pakistan as Bach Hospital had acquired two new doctors, Bev Feldman to help Phyliss with the female patients and Hans Martin Killgaas to do general surgery and to learn eye surgery for planned trips to the extreme north of the country to remote Chitral where almost no medical treatment of any sort was available. There was also a temporary shortage of nurses, so I had convinced one of the local nurses, Vel Reid, who often helped me with eye surgery to accompany Margaret and me on such a mission trip. Vel had collected several pieces of equipment, including fifty sets of sterile pediatric intravenous tubing, pieces of eye sutures, and a few intraocular lenses to take along. I had selected the instruments we would need plus a movie projector that our friends in Pakistan needed and had requested we bring.

With so many supplies in addition to our clothes, we were definitely overweight, and if our bags were inspected and the packages opened, the sterility might be ruined, making them useless, causing us to trust in God that He would take charge of our bags on this trip. Getting to London was no problem, but we prayed hard as we approached the Pakistani inspector at Heathrow airport to board the Pakistani International Airways jet. I explained we were taking medical supplies for use in his country and for his people. He waved us through, not even asking us to open a single bag.

We had spent two days in London sightseeing before traveling on. We three boarded the DC-10 aircraft and selected window seats that were three abreast instead of the five seated center sections. The Pakistanis filled the center seats, changed seats frequently, stuffed the overhead bins and under seat spaces with all sorts of carry on luggage, and created considerable confusion for the attendants.

Once airborne, we were offered the choice of a Pakistani dinner or a European one, then all were served the Pakistani meal of rice pilau and minced meat, very tasty and similar to what we had experienced on our previous trip. For dessert we had rice pudding topped with a square of very thin silver metal. We had seen this being prepared in India as men took a small ball of silver metal and beat it between two pieces of leather to produce a feathery thin sheet. Hindus eat this wrapped over sweets because they believe it gives them added strength. It plays havoc with metallic tooth fillings.

Just after dawn we landed at the oil rich Arab city of Abu Dahbi, where new cars buzzed by the airport and new construction could be seen everywhere. Transferred to a smaller plane, we left there for Islamabad, sister city and neighbor to the older Rawalpindi. Two lines were forming at the customs office, a longer one for Pakistanis and a shorter one for Europeans. Choosing the shorter line, we were whisked through without questions. If our bags had been inspected, we would have been charged a fortune for the medical supplies and the movie projector. God was still on the job. Our friend, Russell Irwin was there to meet us with a big smile and relief that this time I had no rifle over my shoulder.

The same Volkswagen van we had known in 1973 was loaded, and we drove the eighty miles to Bach Hospital. Vel, not having experienced traffic in this part of the world, held tightly to her seat and was speechless as we dodged colorful painted busses, small fast cars, cyclists, people and animals in the road. The drive really became hazardous as darkness fell. One truck, squarely in the road, was up on blocks awaiting two wheels that had been taken for repairs. There were no lights or flares to warn of the danger, but we were able to leave the pavement to avoid hitting a bus that suddenly stopped. Luckily there were no ditches or rocks in the shoulder. Vel was wrung out emotionally by the time we arrived at our destination.

Phyliss met us at the gate and introduced Vel to Nancy, a two year recruit with operating room experience, who would be her roommate. The same cook we had known from our previous trip, Sher (meaning lion in Urdu) got supper ready quickly as we relaxed and unpacked.

The cry "Allah Akbar" (God is Great) calling the Muslims to prayer, awakened us at 5:00 a.m. I had been told the clinic would not begin early, so I went back to sleep. At nine o'clock, Don DeHart, one of the evangelists at the hospital, awakened me to say that seventy-five patients were awaiting "the doctor sahib." When I finally finished clinic at 5:30 p.m. I had seen one hundred five patients and scheduled twenty for surgery the next day and fifteen for later in the week. Only twenty patients could be admitted that first day because that was all the empty beds and the tents had not yet been erected in the yard.

Vel spent the first day working with Nancy to prepare the eye instruments for use. Margaret had visited the wards with Phyliss and taken notes on charts.

The surgery day started, as were many that followed, with an infant who had bilateral congenital cataracts. The two needle irrigation aspiration technique was easy and worked well on these babies. It is vital to regain vision before the age of six because eyes that remain blind until then results in failure of the retinal cells to mature and successful surgery after that date is never able to restore useful vision to the child.

I tried to remove the cataracts intact, but occasionally the anterior capsule ruptures and the lens material must be removed by irrigation and aspiration as in the infants. With the posterior capsule in place and intact, I was able to insert an intraocular lens. These patients would be surprised to be able to see without glasses, unlike most of the others. We were finished with twenty cataracts and two pterygiums by two o'clock. Vel was catching on fast and saved bits of suture material by switching it carefully from one case to the next while still sterile. Repeated heat sterilization weakens it too much.

Ruth Arvidson, a skilled operating room nurse we had worked with on our prior trip, helped again and invited us to have lunch with her. After a much needed siesta, I played ping pong with Russ. I had not played ping pong in several years, and Russ was kind enough not to trounce me badly.

Making rounds on the port op patients the next morning, we thanked God that everyone was fine and our surgery was off to a good start. If I thought the big rush would occur the first clinic day, I was wrong. One hundred patients awaited me next morning as I started, and another twenty five came after lunch. Margaret made eye shields for post op patients and checked the new admissions that afternoon.

A few tents had been erected, and in the afternoon a big storm started in the mountains, but fortunately in never reached the hospital. Patients in the tents were thankful for that.

In surgery the next day, I started teaching Hans Martin cataract surgery. He watched the morning cases and began to do some in the afternoon. He began to learn pretty fast.

Wanting to limit the Saturday morning clinic to fifty patients, we found sixty had come before dawn, so we decided to take them all. There were fifty patients to see on rounds in the afternoon. All the hospital beds were full and several patients and families resided in the rented tents in the yard. Because of our limitations, we had to refuse patients with a cataract in only one eye, if the other was still pretty good. In America we operate eyes with 20/40 vision in the cataract eye and 20/20 in the other.

I saw only a few patients with senile macular degeneration, a common condition in America, but maybe because not as many people attain old age in Pakistan.

Russ drove us to Abbottabad in the afternoon, allowing us frequent stops for photography of such scenes as men treading grain, winnowing wheat, and working in the fields. High mountains, blue skies and white clouds formed wonderful backgrounds for our pictures.

In the city we walked around looking in the shops and being looked at in turn by the people who were curious of us, although the girls wore scarves on their heads and wore pantaloons to cover their legs. Two mental cases were being allowed to roam the streets because only violent ones could take up limited hospital beds. One man, wearing only a long nightgown type garment, would pull up the bottom to expose his private parts to full view, but no one seemed to take notice. One crazy woman grasped the door of a bus and had to be pried loose by police. She was allowed to walk away by herself.

We refreshed ourselves with tea at a tea shop where the waiter got down his best china from an upper shelf to serve us. Our bill was thirty cents for six cups of tea.

The surgery patients are remarkable. They wait their turn without complaint, take their novocaine injections without murmur, and lie very still for their surgery as well as in their beds for as long as necessary after surgery. One man developed a hemorrhage from the retrobulbar injection, resulting in cancellation of the surgery. Having cataracts in both eyes, he asked to have the other one done, so we dilated that pupil and kept him on the list for the other eye. He later said that was the eye he wanted done first anyway. Another patient had gone to Taxila on the wrong day for cataract surgery. When told there was an eye surgeon at Bach, he came and asked us to remove his cataract. We put him on the list and fulfilled his wish.

Making rounds on patients after surgery was much fun. I had a team of seven helpers. One removed the eye pad, another read the chart to be sure we had the right patient, I examined the eye with a special strong flashlight, another writes my comments on the chart, Vel instills the necessary eye drops, and another places a new bandage on the eye. Someone else carries a bowl of antiseptic hand rinse for me to use between patients and one acts as interpreter. There are often one or two extras along for the show. Patients who have healed sufficiently are allowed to go home.

Ruth announced that two hundred new patients had showed up at the clinic. She had only given fifty appointments, but I was able to take thirty more before lunch. More were seen in the afternoon, plus I did more complete examinations on some of the staff members.

It is difficult to explain glaucoma surgery to the patients. If they are already blind in one eye, they want that eye operated on, but that will do no good. I try to explain that the other eye which still sees needs the surgery, but they think I must be mistaken. They say they will think about it and come back, but they never do. I was able to do a trabeculectomy on the only seeing eye of one woman who kept insisting that I was operating on the wrong eye. She wanted the blind eye to be fixed. Glaucoma is a medical disease in America usually where patients can obtain and use therapeutic eye drops for years, but there is no chance of that in Pakistan. Glaucoma, once diagnosed is a surgical disease there.

There was a great fuss at the clinic one morning as three hundred fifty patients arrived and wanted to be examined. Ruth was able to calm things by giving one hundred appointments each day. I was in no danger of being idle for lack of opportunity to serve.

In the nearby village of Manserha where we had gone to buy some small brass bells to take home and some supplies for the hospital, we visitors, with one experienced nurse to guide us, decided to risk a bus ride the six miles back to the hospital. The busses, as well as the trucks, are all decorated with painted scenes on every available space. At each stop, they fill fast and when every seat and all the room in the aisle is filled, they take off, leaving the rest of the would be passengers to await the next bus. Women may only sit with another woman or a husband or close male relative. There is considerable moving about to get the proper seating arrangements. In the cities, people even hang onto the outside of the bus when they have only a short distance to travel. We managed to get off at the correct stop. Bus fare was only a nickel.

After examining the one hundred appointments on Saturday, we packed the VW for an excursion up the Kaghan Valley to see the mountains. To gain the first fifteen miles as the crow flies requires thirty five miles of twisting road. We were able to see the massive Hindu Kush range, an extension of the mighty Himalayas. We passed a couple of camel caravans moving south for the winter season. We traversed several switch backs on a narrow dirt road with no guard rail and serious steep mountain sides drop-offs to gain more altitude. Driving five miles, we attained an elevation of 7000 feet but only about 700 yards farther north. We reached the rest house at Shogran and took rooms for the night. A strenuous climb on foot to the nearest peak gave us a majestic view of the mountains above and the valley below. Dark clouds above a clear section of sky below gave a vivid sunset like streaks of red fire.

The exertion of the climb and hazards of the drive up caused us to sleep well in our sleeping bags that night. The trip home the next day was much easier than the route up.

Monday morning was surgery again. There was a short period when the lights went out. Margaret held the flashlight while I finished the case I was working on. The lights returned soon thereafter.

That afternoon Phyliss asked me to examine a year old baby who was having breathing trouble. My ENT training was very helpful as I made the diagnosis of a tracheal foreign body. By the slimmest chance, the hospital had a small size bronchoscope and a forceps to fit it. We put the baby enough to sleep for me to insert the bronchoscope and find a kernel of corn in the trachea. Grasping it was not too difficult, but the kernel was too big to extract through the scope. It was time for prayer as

I brought the foreign object out trailing the scope. The forceps held firmly and the baby's life was saved. I had three reasons to thank God for a favorable outcome. First, that I knew how to handle the bronchoscope and forceps. Second, that the hospital had such an instrument handy, and third, that the operation was successful.

Hans Martin continued to improve with his cataract surgery, and by the time I left, I felt he would have success on his trips to Chitral.

That evening we all had a party with everyone in cleverly devised costumes. There were skits and songs and Russ did an imitation of me doing surgery and making rounds that brought much laughter and applause.

After our last day of surgery, Margaret gave us a final count: two hundred thirty one major operations and four minor cases, a total of 235. God had even blessed us with a success rate of 97.5%. We had used up all the special supplies we had brought, and we were happy to have been of some help to people who needed so much.

As a special treat we were invited to supper at the home of the one optician in Abbottabad to thank us for the increased business we had sent his way with the several glasses prescriptions we had given. Mr. Qureshi let us sit in chairs and even allowed his wife to sit at table with us. We were served rice pilau, curried meat, chicken, spinach, sliced tomato, onions, radishes and bread. It was an elegant and delicious meal.

November 1 was a day for change of time, starting the winter schedule. Clocks were set back one hour but the mullahs, which were probably recorded, gave out their cry of "Allah, Akbar" at five o'clock the old time. There were also speeches telling the hospital patients not to read our tracts or listen to the preaching by the Christian evangelists. Patients were willing to accept our medical help, but didn't want any spiritual help.

Russ and Phyliss had planned a special adventure to top off our stay, a trip to the extreme north to the "nation" of Swat. The national government had very little administration in Swat, but allowed the local "king" nearly full authority. The present ruler's father was the real "King of Swat," not referring to Babe Ruth, however. Leaving the post-op patients in the hands of the now fairly capable Hans Martin, we felt comfortable being away four days. Phyliss had left Bev Feldman in charge of the regular hospital patients.

We drove northwest to Haripur, then plunged into a mountain range that appeared to have no opening but found one narrow gorge with one narrow road winding upward. Up and up we climbed in numerous switch backs that brought us much higher, but no farther north. Finally we reached the Tarbela Dam, largest earthen dam in the world, two miles across, 500 feet high and one mile thick at its base, behind which a huge blue lake had formed. We crossed the dam and had a nice picnic lunch in the slightly warm sunshine. Going over one more mountain, we reached Saidu Sharif, where a proper hotel was found for the night.

The Swat Valley narrowed more and more until it became a tight stony gorge with a river rushing down it. On one wider, calmer part of the river was a raft made of four goat skins sewn together, legs sticking upward, on which people were being ferried across. Though quite comical, the contraption was functional. Beside the road and the river was an old wooden mosque, intricately and handsomely carved. As we ate a picnic lunch on the rocky shore, we saw a troupe of two dozen wild monkeys across the river, searching for worms or grubs in the grass or under the rocks.

Farther up the valley, the road became impassable, and there we encountered a marble palace where the former Wali (ruler or king) had lived and ruled almost supreme until his death. His son, the present owner, had neither the authority nor the wealth of the father as Pakistan had extended its rule more completely over the area. Colorful shops lined the narrow road and we enjoyed walking along inspecting the goods being displayed in the open front booths.

At tea time, we ate local hamburgers of ground meat patties cooked in bubbling grease, after the flies had been brushed away, along with onions and red peppers. The meat balls were inserted into chapatis (round flat bread like naan). We reasoned that the germs had been killed by the boiling grease. The peppers were a little hot for our western palates, but fairly mild by Pakistani standards.

Turning toward home, we followed the river to where it joined the larger Indus River to the Attock Fort, where an old, two decker bridge crossed the river, the upper deck for trains and the lower for cars. Larger trucks could not negotiate the sharp turn required to get on the bridge, so a new bridge was being constructed. Extending only one forth across, it had been being built for five years, so we thought it would be a long time before completion.

The Kabul River from Afghanistan joined at this point to swell the Indus into a big, wide stream.

We encountered a police road block where truck drivers had their licenses inspected and overloaded busses were being stopped. Truck drivers warned others approaching about the barricade, and those without licenses, of which there were many, pulled off the road to await clearing of the inspection site before proceeding on. Busses had to wait for hours or unload some passengers before continuing. Private cars were not being detained, so we drove on. After a few hours, the police moved to another location, and the traffic resumed.

When we arrived back at the hospital, we praised Russ for his tireless and skillful driving and thanked God for His ever watchful care of us.

The time came all too soon for our departure and the drive to Islamabad. On the way we stopped once more at Taxila to see Norval Christy and the eye hospital there.

With the year nearly over, the team had done over 9000 cataract operations and were headed for a record year.

We had time for a short visit and a prayer before going on.

With a final afternoon of shopping in Rawalpindi and an overnight in a vacant missionary home, we drove to the airport in Islamabad early the next day. The baggage Margaret, Vel, and I had accumulated was almost eighty pounds over the limit. The charge was $400. The agent asked me, "How much can you pay?" Searching my pockets, I found a total of $75. With only a moment's hesitation, he wrote a receipt for $70 and said, "You understand?"

Russell replied in Urdu, "We understand very well." Carrying our hand luggage as if it were straw goods and feathers, we thanked God that wasn't weighed, and then we bid our friends farewell.

Vel's husband met her at Heathrow to travel back to Florida with her. Margaret and I had decided to stay a bit longer in England, so we left them to pick up a rental car and start on a drive to the Cotswold area for a rest time.

After a night of imperfect sleep because of jet lag, we enjoyed driving through the green, rolling countryside with fat cows in grassy meadows, between hedgerows and country homes.

In Brouton-on-Water, an attractive little tourist town, we took a room in the hotel adjacent to the small stream that flowed through the center of the city and did some leisurely sightseeing. Fifty years ago, the villagers had built a model of the town to the scale of one tenth size. Little paths were present for walking through the model town and there was even a smaller model of the model town built to yet another one tenth scale.

A butterfly museum was an interesting stop for us. The colorful insects had been gathered from many parts of the world and were allowed to fly about inside the wire enclosure for their short lives of two to four months, then they were mounted on pins for permanent display.

We spent a pleasant three days driving around the Cotswolds, visiting the various cathedrals and churches with stained glass windows. In one was a statue of Dr. Edward Jenner, discoverer of smallpox vaccine. In the Glouster cathedral is a small stained glass window depicting a medieval golfer striking a ball. Postcards of the window and wooden copies were being sold to tourists.

On our way back to Heathrow we went by the city of Tunbridge Wells to see our missionary friends from Afghanistan, who, being sent out of the country, had returned to England to work in the National Health Service. We ate supper with Howard and Monika Harper and their three daughters, Naomi, Faith, and Joy at the Rose and Crown Restaurant, a typical pleasant British pub.

Our flight home landed in Boston, where customs clearance was much easier than New York. A planned stop in Atlanta gave us a chance to visit our daughter, Janet and her husband Larry, and also our son, Dudley and his wife Patty. We had a splendid dinner at a restaurant in the top floor of the tall Hilton Hotel in downtown Atlanta. Patty and Larry had birthdays the next day, which was also Margaret and my wedding anniversary, so we celebrated all three events by having a specially baked soufflé for each.

We returned to Fort Lauderdale the next day. We had so much to give thanks to God for regarding another trip where I was trying to give back to God but in doing so derived much more coming back to me than I had given. Again I learned that I can't out give God.

1979

The Lighthouse for Christ in Mombasa, Kenya, where our son Dudley had made his Christian commitment, was asking for someone to relieve the founder and director, Dr. Bill Ghrist, while he returned to America for a medical check up and rest period. This was a good opportunity to travel and work again with our friends Dr. Al and Libby Smith and to take nurse Vel Reid on a second trip. Vel had convinced her friend Mae Sorenson to accompany her and us. With adequate help and no excess need or demand for service, this trip had every expectation of being productive but not back-breaking, rewarding and refreshing with time for consultation and reflection on our mission.

Al and Libby and Margaret and I were in Nairobi when Vel and Mae arrived with plans to rest a day before proceeding on to Mombasa. We four went on ahead to prepare for the arrival of the nurses the next day. A volunteer worker with Campus Crusade for Christ, Kathy Larkins, met us at the small, calm Mombasa airport and drove us in a VW bus to the Eye Center, located on a bluff overlooking the harbor and the city. It was late September, still summer there on the equator, but a pleasant breeze off the Indian Ocean was very comfortable.

With both Bill and June Ghrist away and only John, the local house keeper, cook and weekend preacher in residence, we spent the first day getting organized. The clinic manager, Philip, and his wife, Julietta, supervisor of the operating room, came to greet us and prepare for their duties. We went grocery shopping in the afternoon and gathered Vel and Mae at the airport when they arrived, excited at the prospects of their adventure. Around the supper table, we made plans for our work. Patients were scheduled to arrive the next morning for clinic.

Patients arrived early, were seated in the large reception area, and were lectured about the clinic and the purpose for its existence as an outreach of Christian concern for the world. John took over this function in June's absence. Al and I arranged our examination instruments and shared seeing the two dozen patients before noon and a similar number after lunch. Most were patients for routine eye care and there was not near as much pathology as we had seen in Afghanistan. There was time in the late afternoon to sit in the yard some hundred feet above the harbor and watch the sun go down as boat traffic moved slowly in the water below.

There were only three cataract surgeries the first operating day, but they were all complicated cases requiring an iridectomy or breaking of synechiae or teasing out a hypermature lens. Vel and Mae had prepared our instruments well and were skillful help in the surgery. Al and I were distressed by the dimness of the operating light and spent some time trying to improve it. We finally realized the problem lay at the source, the electricity power supply, and it could only be helped a little. We improved the illumination by adding a floor lamp and our visibility by increasing our magnifying loupes.

All six of us went to the Nyali Beach Hotel in the late afternoon to swim in the hotel pool and walk in the fine white sand of the beach. We ate chicken and shrimp curry for supper in the restaurant.

Our first weekend was free for an excursion to nearby Tsavo Park for a two night stay at the Kilaguni Lodge and game viewing in the Park. A large water hole behind the lodge attracted different groups at different times and the dining room and veranda offered good viewing sites. Nearly two dozen elephants had arrived that first afternoon. Mt. Kilimanjaro is visible to the south and was a beautiful scene in the light of the setting sun. We were treated to a lecture about the park and animals that evening. Floodlights over the pool revealed several cape buffalo who came to drink later in the night.

Early the next morning we drove a few miles to Mzima Springs, where fresh water bubbles up from the lava rock to begin a flow that becomes the Tsavo River. The springs also serves as the water supply for the city of Mombasa by way of a pipe line. Several hippos live in the pool and two young males put on a show of mouth wrestling which we photographed. The water was so clear that we could watch the monstrous beasts paddling under the surface. They frequently break the surface with their nose, eyes and ears to survey their surroundings. I was reminded of my first safari when I had paddled down the Tana River being careful not to get too close to the hippos and get upended by one coming up under our boat.

On our drive out to the springs and back we saw elephant, oryx, kongoni, giraffe, buffalo, and several impala. The light brown antelope are such graceful runners and leapers that they are fun to watch in action.

Back at the lodge for lunch, we met two families who know medical friends of ours in Miami and also know Dr. Herb Friesen in Afghanistan. The world is pretty small after all. Zebra and impala came to the water hole while we ate the buffet lunch.

During our afternoon game drive we saw baboons, female ostriches, elephant, impala, kongoni, lesser kudu, and some tiny klipspringers, which climb rocky hills and cling to seemingly impossible places to stand. As we ate supper, the buffalo and elephants returned to the waterhole. Sunday we drove around to see more animals, all familiar to me and Margaret, but new and strange to the nurses.

Monday, back at the Lighthouse, Al and I did more cataract surgeries and examined our post op patients. They were all doing fine.

In the late afternoon we all went to the woodcarvers shed. Hundreds of men work in the open sided huts. Cutting wood, carving likenesses of animals or native faces. This is a real industry where the men get skilled at carving certain animals which they repeat again and again, becoming quick and good. The pieces are sold in many tourist shops. We bought some for home and ordered a number of small lambs to be made for us to send as Christmas gifts. A big sign informs visitors that it is illegal to buy pieces directly from the workers, but many carvers ignore the notice and offer their carvings as the "best price."

Supper was a real treat, African rock lobster tails and shrimp creole on rice. We seemed to be doing as much vacationing as working, unlike most of our previous trips when we worked very hard.

After seeing all the clinic patients the next day, we all went to a beach on the south Kenya coast, reached by a ferry trip from Mombasa to the mainland. Obtaining rooms in a hotel, we put on our swim suits and walked on the beach whose sand was extremely smooth and white, much like baby powder. As the sun set over the Indian Ocean, we lounged on the hotel veranda in the cool breeze and enjoyed sundowners. The following morning we hired a glass bottom boat to view the reefs off shore, taking snorkels, flippers and face masks to enter the underwater world where we saw fish of all varied colors and sizes as we swam around the corals. Brilliant red starfish, black sea urchins and ugly sea slugs dotted the sandy bottom. Some of the coral was smooth like brains, some lacy like fans and some like fingered hands. We could almost touch the fish as they swam by in a kaleidoscope of patterns.

Returning to the Lighthouse for the afternoon clinic, Al and I were able to see the forty or more patients who awaited our return.

After clinic the next day we six drove to the North Kenya shore to visit the National Marine Park near Malindi. Cashews were in season, and we bought several pounds of the toasted nuts at a cheap price, eating some for snacks and planning for more in the days to follow.

The girls would have no part of the snake handling show scheduled for the evening at the hotel, so we went to our rooms and to bed.

Again snorkeling was available over the reefs in the Park, and we viewed an incredible number and variety of fish. Al and I took bread and fed the fish under the glass bottom boat for the girls to see also. In the afternoon we explored the Arab city of Gedi, which was abandoned some 600 years ago and had been overgrown by jungle until restored in recent years. The city reminded me of Angkor Wat in Cambodia.

The Seafarers Lodge, where we were staying, had an excellent chef, and we ate an outstanding crab and lobster dinner, the best meal of our entire trip.

I enjoyed watching the weaver birds in the trees near the lodge. About the size of a sparrow, the yellow and black weavers build nests that hang down from limbs and stay busy gathering twigs to construct their intricate nests.

On our drive back to the Lighthouse we saw many women of the Giriana tribe. The tall, erect women carry large loads balanced atop their heads, go bare breasted and have an accumulation of fat on their buttocks that jiggle as they walk in almost comical fashion.

Surgery increased and the pathology was more varied the next day. We found evidence of a brain tumor in one patient and a retinal detachment in another. Not having the equipment for retina surgery, we referred the patient to a surgeon in town.

A "bush eye camp" was scheduled for Wednesday, so we loaded the VW with supplies and equipment and drove to the village of Kaioleni, about thirty miles inland. As Al and I examined the eye patients, Vel and Mae went to help the general surgeon, Dr. David Thompson, do a hysterectomy. Dr. Thompson had served over twenty years in China before being expelled and came to Kenya. We did no eye surgery in the village, but referred some patients back to the Lighthouse for further care.

While we were away, the African staff went out witnessing using the four spiritual laws booklet. We returned in time to join their report session with songs and prayer. After another day of clinic patients, Al and Libby left to fly back to Nairobi and home.

Margaret, Vel, Mae and I stayed over Sunday to attend a bush church that John, the cook, pastored. Most of the members of the congregation were children. The teenagers sang songs recited their memory Bible verses or played tambourines or drums. The drummer appeared to be younger than ten, but he had a fine sense of rhythm. We guests were introduced; then John preached. His sermon, translated into English for our benefit, was on tithing, the last thing we expected in such a setting. It was fun taking pictures after the service as the children each wanted to be in the front and kept jockeying for position.

We had time that afternoon for a drive to Shimba Hills National Park to see herds of the beautiful sable antelope that reside there. The sable is a large antelope with scimitar shaped long horns sweeping back over their black shoulders. We also saw roan antelope and a couple of wart hogs that run with their little tails straight up.

I did the surgery the next day with Mae circulating, Vel scrubbing, and Margaret holding the light. We would leave the surgical patients for Dr. Bill Ghrist to care for, as he would be returning soon.

The final day of clinic was pretty full, after which we were invited to "high tea" by a local Ear, Nose and Throat specialist from India, Dr. Ved and his charming wife. "High tea" includes several types of snacks made in typical Indian style, a real taste sensation and conversation stimulus. Margaret enjoys knowing about different types of food.

Passing through Nairobi on our way home, we left our excess baggage and gifts with Peg to be shipped to the States for much less cost than airline overweight charge.

Vel and Mae expressed their delight with the trip and work as we all flew home after yet another splendid mission trip. I had in part paid my debt to God for my medical education and guidance under His mighty hand.

CHAPTER 7
LIVING WATER CARE CENTER

1999 - 2001

God gave me one more chance before I was ready to retire to repay my debt to Him and to the people who were representative of those on whom I had learned my skills.

A section of western Broward County near the Dade County line was surveyed and it was found that 65% of the people living there had no health insurance, no Medicare or Medicaid and little money. After careful consideration and planning, the Gulf Stream Baptist Association decided to open a free medical clinic to offer help. An unused Sunday School building behind a church that had lost a lot of members because of a shifting population was remodeled by a Baptist work team that moves from place to place where needed. It was fully equipped as a clinic. A receptionist was hired, a volunteer nurse found, and it was named the Living Water Care Center.

Arrangements were made for referrals to Hollywood Memorial Hospital for the patients who needed special care the clinic could not offer.

A physician from Miami came as a volunteer the first day the clinic was opened, but decided she could not continue coming once a week without a salary of $25,000 yearly. There was no money for such expenditure, and the clinic was about to close before it really got started.

The assistant minister at my church, First Baptist of Fort Lauderdale, who was on the Gulf Stream Baptist board, asked me if I could help the clinic stay open. I had turned my ophthalmology practice over to a younger doctor and was only working as a refractionist in an optical dispensary three days each week. I agreed to give one day each week while we attempted to get more volunteers. Having had a year of internal medicine at the start of my career and having just taught medical assisting for two years at Fort Lauderdale's City College, I felt confident enough in general medicine to do the job.

The clinic receptionist, Norma Nelson, lived near the clinic and knew the neighborhood well. Soon an internist Dr. Hernandez, a Christian doctor from Venezuela, agreed to come one afternoon, and his charming wife, Maria, a nurse, agreed to work with me all day Thursdays. A pediatrician who had just passed her state board examination agreed to help every other Wednesday. We were soon able to meet the demand and were up and going.

Most of the patients were Cuban or Central American immigrants, so my ability to speak and understand a moderate amount of Spanish was helpful. The clinic also offered me an opportunity to practice medicine in a very satisfying way. I had time to talk to patients about their faith, or lack of it, and to express some of my own faith to them. We had copies of the Gospel of John in Spanish to offer those who might benefit from reading it.

One day a beautiful young teenager was brought in complaining about frequent tiny bruising of her arms. She carried a flag in the school marching bank and twirled the banner around as part of her performance. Her tiny bruises reminded me of similar bruises in had seen on a young child of family friends. A blood count revealed a severe shortage of blood platelets, a condition called thrombocytopenia. We arranged for a couple of transfusions of blood components at the University of Miami Hospital, which corrected the condition.

After the clinic had been in operation a year, the Gulf Stream Baptist Association rented a big tent, erected it on the spacious yard next to the clinic and gave a luncheon to which they invited several community leaders and prominent citizens of the area, one of which was the mayor of Hollywood. The clinic had won a community award for service from the Broward County Health Department after our first year of operation.

I was enjoying the variety of patients I was seeing and treating. We had accumulated a nice supply of sample medicine, given to the clinic by a nurse from my church who worked for three physicians and collected a wide assortment of samples.

The second year of our operation, a semiretired dentist got interested in the clinic and donated a chair and equipment. We converted one room into a dental office and he recruited two other dentists to help in that much needed area.

When I retired and moved to Knoxville, Tennessee, at the end of my third year with the clinic, the Living Water Care Center was busy every day of the week with four doctors and two dentists. I left things in good hands and felt that God had given me one last chance to repay the debt lowed to my heavenly Father and the type people who had helped me get started in a very satisfying career.

TATE PUBLISHING, LLC

127 East Trade Center Terrace
Mustang, Oklahoma 73064

(888) 361 - 9473

TATE PUBLISHING, LLC
www.tatepublishing.com